Ernest Chester Thomas

Leading Cases in constitutional Law briefly stated

Ernest Chester Thomas

Leading Cases in constitutional Law briefly stated

ISBN/EAN: 9783337187767

Printed in Europe, USA, Canada, Australia, Japan

Cover: Foto ©ninafisch / pixelio.de

More available books at **www.hansebooks.com**

LEADING CASES

IN

CONSTITUTIONAL LAW

BRIEFLY STATED.

WITH INTRODUCTION AND NOTES.

BY

ERNEST C. THOMAS, Esq.,

LATE SCHOLAR OF TRINITY COLLEGE, OXFORD, AND BACON SCHOLAR
OF THE HON. SOCIETY OF GRAY'S INN.

JUDICIA ENIM ANCORAE LEGUM SUNT UT LEGES REIPUBLICAE.

SECOND EDITION.

LONDON:

STEVENS & HAYNES,

Law Publishers,

BELL YARD, TEMPLE BAR.

1885.

LONDON
BRADBURY, AGNEW, & CO. LD., PRINTERS, WHITEFRIARS.

PREFACE

TO THE SECOND EDITION.

I NEED only say by way of introduction to the present edition, that the demand for this little book during the time it has been out of print has been such as to convince me, that it has been found useful to those for whose use it was originally published, and is now again committed to the press.

A sufficient explanation of the design of this work will be found in the following paragraphs, which I repeat here from the Preface to the First Edition.

"Some knowledge of the chief cases in Constitutional Law is now required in many examinations, and is obviously necessary to the thorough student of our constitutional history. Yet there has existed no book briefly setting out the main principles decided in these cases, which are scattered through many volumes, and buried in prolix reports. Even Dr. Broom's book, although, in spite of its thousand pages, it is the nearest approach to anything of the kind, lacks the brevity and conciseness which are so necessary for the student.

"What I have endeavoured to do is to extract the essence of the cases with which the student is expected to be familiar, preserving always something of the concrete circumstance that is so helpful to the memory; to add, where necessary, a short note to the individual case; and to subjoin to each important group of cases some general remarks in the shape of a Note. The cases are so arranged as to be convenient for ready reference, and while the treatment is very concise, I hope that it is sufficiently accurate."

The technical way in which legal arguments are conducted in Court, and the fact that students usually take up the study of Constitutional History and Law before they have learnt how to find their way among the innumerable volumes of the reports, make a convenient guide to them the more necessary. But it need hardly be added that the student should by no means neglect to examine for himself the reports "at large."

E. C. T.

3, HARCOURT BUILDINGS, TEMPLE,
January, 1885.

TABLE OF CONTENTS.

	PAGE
PREFACE	v
AUTHORITIES QUOTED, with Abbreviations	x
TABLE OF CASES summarised or cited	xiv
INTRODUCTION	1

LEADING CASES:
The Case of Monopolies	11
The Case of Proclamations	13
Thomas v. Sorrel	14
Godden v. Hales	15
Seven Bishops' Case	16
Bate's Case (Case of Impositions)	20
Rex v. Hampden (Case of Ship money)	23
NOTE I.—On the Dispensing Power	26
Barnardiston v. Soame	28
Ashby v. White	30
Case of Lord Shaftesbury	33
Rex v. Eliot, Hollis and Valentine	34
Rex v. Lord Abingdon	36
Rex v. Creevey	37
Burdett v. Abbot	38
Stockdale v. Hansard	40
Sheriff of Middlesex's Case	42
Howard v. Gosset	43
Bradlaugh v. Erskine	44
Bradlaugh v. Gosset	45
NOTE II.—On Privilege of Parliament and the Law Courts	46
Calvin's Case	48
NOTE III.—On Allegiance and Aliens	49

	PAGE
Campbell v. Hall	50
Bankers' Case	51
Viscount Canterbury v. The Attorney-General	52
Tobin v. The Queen	53
The Queen v. The Lords Commissioners of the Treasury	54
NOTE IV.—On Remedies against the Crown	55
Darnel's Case (Five Knights' Case)	57
Shanley v. Harvey	58
Sommersett's Case	59
Forbes v. Cochrane	60
Case of Le Louis	61
Case of the Slave Grace	62
Pigg v. Caley	63
Rex v. Broadfoot	65
Wilkes v. Wood	67
Leach v. Money	68
Entick v. Carrington	69
NOTE V.—On General Warrants	70
Lane v. Cotton	72
Macbeath v. Haldimand	73
Gidley v. Lord Palmerston	74
Grant v. Secretary of State for India	75
Fabrigas v. Mostyn	76
Cameron v. Kyte	77
Hill v. Bigge	78
Phillips v. Eyre	79
Musgrave v. Pulido	80
Tandy v. Earl of Westmoreland	81
Luby v. Lord Wodehouse	82
Sullivan v. Earl Spencer	83
NOTE VI.—On the Liability of Governors	84
Grant v. Sir Charles Gould	86
Sutton v. Johnstone	87
Dawkins v. Lord Rokeby	88
Madrazo v. Willes	90
Buron v. Denman	91
NOTE VII.—On the Liability of Officers—Military and Naval	92
Prohibitions del Roy (Case of Prohibitions)	94
Floyd v. Barker	95

Table of Contents.

	PAGE
Bushell's Case	96
Hamond v. Howell	97
Houlden v. Smith	98
Kemp v. Neville	99
Fray v. Blackburn	100
Calder v. Halket	101
Note VIII.—On the Liability of Judges	102
Astley v. Younge	104
Munster v. Lamb	105
Seaman v. Netherclift	106
Wason v. Walter	108
Curry v. Walter	109
Usill v. Hales	110
Davison v. Duncan	111

APPENDIX.
Attorney-General v. Bradlaugh 112

INDEX 115–123

AUTHORITIES QUOTED.

WITH THE ABBREVIATIONS USED.

Adolphus & Ellis, King's Bench Reports, 1834-41, 12 vols. . . . . Ad. & E.
Barnewell & Alderson, King's Bench Reports, 1817-22, 5 vols. . . . B. & Ald.
Barnewell & Cresswell, King's Bench Reports, 1822-30, 10 vols. . . . B. & C.
Best & Smith, Queen's Bench Reports, 1861-69, 10 vols. . . . . . B. & S.
Blackstone, Henry, Reports . . . H. Bl.
Blackstone, Sir W., Commentaries on the Law of England, 15th ed., 4 vols. . . . Comm.
Broderip & Bingham, Common Pleas, &c., Reports, 1819-23, 3 vols. . . . Brodr. & B.
Broom, H., Constitutional Law, 1866 . . Br.
Burrow, Reports . . . . . Burr.

Campbell, Lord, Lives of the Chancellors, 8 vols., 8vo . . . . Camp. Chanc.
Campbell, Lord, Lives of the Chief Justices, 3 vols. 8vo.
Campbell, Reports . . . . Campb.
Carrington & Marshman, Reports . . Carr. & M.
Chitty, Reports . . . . . . Chitty.
Clarendon, Lord, Hist. of the Rebellion, Oxford, 1849, 7 vols., 8vo.
Coke, Institutes . . . . . Coke, Inst.
Coke, Reports . . . . . . Rep.
Common Bench Reports, New Series, 20 vols. . . . . . . C. B. N. S.

Authorities Quoted.

Cowper, Reports . . . . . Cowp.
Cox, H., Institutions of the English
 Government . . . . . Cox, Inst. Engl. Gov.
Croke, Reports (Charles I.) . . . Cro. Car.

Dodson, Admiralty Reports, 2 vols. . . Dods. Adm. R.
Dow, Reports, 6 vols. . . . . Dow.
Dyer, Reports . . . . . . Dyer.

East, King's Bench Reports . . . East.
Eden, Chancery Reports . . . Eden.
Ellis & Blackburn, Reports . . E. & B.
Ellis, Blackburn, & Ellis, Reports . . E., B. & E.
Espinasse, Nisi Prius Reports. . . Esp.
Exchequer Reports . . . . . Exch.

Forsyth, Cases and Opinions in Constitu-
 tional Law, 1869.
Foster, Crown Law . . . . Foster.
Foster & Finlason, Reports. . . . F. & F.
Freeman, Reports, K. B.

Gardiner, S. R., History of England,
 1603-1642, 10 vols.

Haggard, Admiralty Reports . . . Hagg. Adm. R.
Hallam, Constitutional History of Eng-
 land, 7th ed., 8vo, 3 vols. . . . Hall. C. H. E.
Hearn, Government of England, 1867 . Gov. Engl.

Irish Common Law Reports . . . Ir. C. L. R.
Irish Reports . . . . . . I. R.

Knapp, Privy Council Cases . . . Knapp, P. C. C.

Law Journal . . . . . . L. J.
Law Reports, 1865 . . . . . L. R.
Law Times Reports . . . . . L. T.
Lofft, Reports . . . . . Lofft.

Mason's Reports (U.S.) . . . . Mason.
Maule & Selwyn, Reports . . . M. & S.
May, Constitutional History of England . May, C. H. E.
May, Parliamentary Practice, 9th ed. . May, P. P.
Meeson & Welsby, Reports . . . M. & W.

Authorities Quoted.

Modern Reports	Mod.
Moore, Privy Council Cases	Moo. P. C. C.
Morison's Dictionary of Decisions (Scotch)	Mor. Dict.
Noy, Reports	Noy.
Parliamentary History	Parl. Hist.
Phillips, Reports, 2 vols.	Phill.
Phillips, State Trials prior to 1688, 2 vols. 1826	Phill. S. T.
Queen's Bench Reports, 18 vols.	Q. B.
Raymond, Lord, Reports, 3 vols.	Lord Raymond.
Rushworth's Historical Collections	Rushw.
Shower, Cases in Parliament	Show. P. C.
Shower, Reports	Show.
Siderfin, Reports	Sid.
Skinner, Reports	Skinn.
Smith, Leading Cases, 8th ed.	Smith, L. C.
Starkie, Reports	Stark.
State Trials : ed. Howell, 34 vols., 1809–26	S. T.
Stephen, Sir J. F., History of the Criminal Law, 3 vols.	Hist.
Taswell-Langmead, Constitutional History, 2nd ed., 1880	Tasw.-Langm. C. H.
Term Reports	T. R.
Todd, Parliamentary Government in England, 2 vols., 1867	Todd, Parl. Gov.
Vaughan, Reports, fol.	Vaughan.
Weekly Reporter	W. R.
Wheaton's Reports (U.S.)	Wheaton.
Wilson, Reports, 3 vols.	Wils.

OTHER ABBREVIATIONS ARE:

L. C. J., Lord Chief Justice of the King's, or Queen's, Bench.
C. J., Chief Justice of the Common Pleas.
L. J., Lord Justice of Appeal.
J., Mr. Justice.
C. B., Lord Chief Baron.
B., Mr. Baron.
H. L., House of Lords.
P. C., Privy Council.
Sc. Cam., or S. C. (Scaccarii Camera), Exchequer Chamber.
Q. B., Queen's Bench.
C. P., Common Pleas.
Ch. Div., Chancery Division; Ex., Exchequer; Ex. Div., Exchequer Division; Ch. D., Chancery Division; Q. B. D., Queen's Bench Division.
A.-G., Attorney-General.
S.-G., Solicitor-General.

TABLE OF CASES

SUMMARIZED OR CITED.

* *The principal Cases are printed in Italics.*

	PAGE
Antelope, The . . .	61
Ashby v. White . .	130
Astley v. Younge . . .	104
Attorney-General v. Bradlaugh	112
'Aylesbury Men' . .	31
Bankers' Case . . .	51
Barnardiston v. Soame .	28
Barwis v. Keppel . .	93
Bate's Case	20
Bradlaugh v. Erskine .	44
——— *Gosset* . .	45
Brook v. Montague . .	106
Burdett v. Abbot . .	38
Buron v. Denman . .	91
Butler v. Crouch . .	63
Calder v. Halket . . .	101
Calvin's Case . . .	48
Cameron v. Kyte . . .	77
Campbell v. Hall . .	50
Canterbury v. Att.-Gen. .	52
Case of Eton College .	26
——— Impositions . .	20
——— Monopolies . .	11
——— Proclamations . .	13
——— Prohibitions . .	94
——— the Seven Bishops	16
——— Lord Shaftesbury .	33
Craw v. Ramsey . .	48

	PAGE
Crouch's Case . . .	63
Cullen v. Morris . .	32
Currey v. Walter . . .	109
Damport v. Sympson .	106
Darnel's Case . . .	57
Davison v. Duncan . .	37
Dawkins v. Lord Rokeby .	88
——————— *Paulet* .	89
Doe d. Thomas v. Acklam	49
Doyle v. Falconer . .	38
Dutton v. Howell . .	85
East India Co. v. Sandys .	11
Entick v. Carrington .	69
Fabrigas v. Mostyn . .	76
Feather v. The Queen . .	12
Fenton v. Hampton . .	38
Five Knights' Case . .	57
Flewster v. Royle . .	66
Fleyer v. Crouch . . .	63
Floyd v. Barker . . .	95
Forbes v. Cochrane . .	60
Fox, *Ex parte* . . .	66
Fray v. Blackburn . .	100
Gidley v. Lord Palmerston	74
Godden v. Hales . .	15
Goffin v. Donnelly . .	107
Grant v. Gould . .	80

Table of Cases.

	PAGE		PAGE
Grant v. Secretary of State for India	75	Palmer v. Hutchinson	74
Hammond v. Howell	97	Pappa v. Rose	102
Harvey v. Lord Aylmer	84	Phillips v. Eyre	79
Hettihewage Siman Appu v. Queen's Advocate	74	Pigg v. Caley	63
Hill v. Bigge	78	Prideaux v. Morrice	29
Hodgkinson v. Fernie	92	Proclamations, Case of	13
Hodgson v. Scarlett	106	Prohibitions, Case of	94
Houlden v. Smith	98	Purcell v. Sowler	111
Howard v. Gosset	43		
Jewison v. Dyson	39	Queen v. The Commissioners of Inland Revenue	56
		Queen v. Lords Commissioners of the Treasury	54
Kemp v. Neville	99		
Kielly v. Carson	38		
King v. Lords of the Treasury	56	Reg. v. Eyre	85
Knight v. Wedderburn	59	Rex v. Broadfoot	65
		—— Creevey	37
		—— Eliot, Hollis and Valentine	34
La Jeune Eugénie	61	—— Hampden	23
Lane v. Cotton	72	—— Hobhouse	42
Leach v. Money	68	—— Lord Abingdon	36
Le Louis	61	—— Picton	85
Lines v. Lord Charles Russell	43	—— Skinner	95
Luby v. Lord Wodehouse	82	—— Tubbs	66
		—— Wall	85
Macbeath v. Haldimand	73		
Macclesfield, Earl of, v. Starkey	95	Scott v. Stansfield	98
Madrazo v. Willes	90	Seven Bishops' Case	16
Monopolies, Case of	11	Shaftesbury's Case, Lord	33
Munster v. Lamb	105	Shanley v. Harvey	58
Musgrave v. Pulido	88	Sheriff of Middlesex's Case	42
		Ship Money, Case of	23
		Slave Grace's Case	62
Neville v. Stroud	28	Sommersett's Case	59
Nicholson v. Mouncey	92	Speaker of Legislative Assembly of Victoria v. Glasse	39
O'Byrne v. Lord Hartington	83	Stockdale v Hansard	40
O'Grady v. Cardwell	74	Sullivan v. Earl Spencer	83
		Sutton v. Johnstone	87

	PAGE		PAGE
Taafe v. Downes	102	Warden v. Bailey	87
Tandy v. Lord Westmoreland	81	Wason v. Walter	108
Thomas v. Churton	89	Whitfield v. Lord le De Spencer	72
——— v. The Queen	53	Wilkes v. Lord Halifax	70
——— v. Sorrel	14	——— v. Wood	67
Tobin v. The Queen	53	Wynne v. Middleton	29
Tozer v. Child	32		
Usill v. Hales	110		

LEADING CASES
IN
CONSTITUTIONAL LAW.

INTRODUCTION.

WHERE there exists a body of laws regulating the distribution and exercise of the supreme power in a community, and a Court entrusted with its interpretation, the term Constitutional Law has a very definite application. That is the case, for example, in the United States. In England, on the other hand, where there is no written constitution, this law exists in a much looser shape, and can only be collected from legal decisions, parliamentary precedents, and actual practice.

Constitutional Law—where to be found.

We are here concerned with constitutional usage only in so far as it has been established or illustrated by the decisions of the law-courts. Although these are far from covering the whole extent of constitutional practice, we shall see that many of the most important principles of the Constitution have come under the discussion and determination of the Courts. That part of our constitutional law should have been made by the judges, will not surprise anyone who knows how enormous has been their influence in the whole field of English law.[1]

Importance of judicial decisions.

For practical purposes we must take the term 'Con-

Constitutional Law—its extent.

---

[1] "The whole of the rules of Equity and nine-tenths of the rules of Common Law have in fact been made by the judges."—*Mellish*, L. J., in *Allen* v. *Jackson*, L. R. 1 Ch. Div. 405.

stitutional Law' to include not only what Austin calls 'constitutional law proper,' but also what he calls 'administrative law,' the two branches making up together 'the law of political conditions, or public law.'[1] Constitutional law proper, in his view, only 'fixes the constitution or structure of the given supreme government.' Administrative law determines the mode in which the sovereign power is to be exercised, either by the sovereign power itself, or by the subordinate political officers to whom portions of the sovereign power may be delegated.

Its object— the prevention and remedy of misgovernment.

Or we may put it in another way perhaps, and say that Constitutional Law has for it object security against misrule, and remedy in the event of misrule. And we shall for the present be chiefly concerned with this latter aspect of constitutional law. We shall consider a particular class of injuries and delinquencies arising from the misuse of the power bestowed upon rulers and administrators, and the remedies provided for them by the tribunals of the country.

Its relation to Common Law misrepresented.

An attempt has been made in one of the few works upon this subject to elaborate a contrast between Constitutional Law and Common Law, and to 'illustrate the relation between them.'[2] Constitutional law is there said to mean 'the aggregate of doctrines and sanctions directly tending to the maintenance of our social union;' and common law, 'the aggregate of rules and maxims directly tending to the maintenance of private rights.' The antithesis here attempted does not really exist; there is no such line of demarcation between constitutional law and common law. They are not disparate and independent branches of law. Constitutional law is simply a portion of the common law, and is included in it as the part is included in the whole. The distinction is not only useless and untrue—it is even dangerous. It

[1] 1 Austin, Jurispr. 4th ed. pp. 73, 274.
[2] Broom, Const. L. pp. vii., viii.

is precisely this notion that the constitutional law was above and beside the common law, that has caused some of the chief difficulties of our constitutional history. It explains not only the exaggerated claims of the Stuart monarchy, with its pretence of a divine authority not subject to the laws, but it also explains the comparatively recent attempt on the part of the House of Commons to assert what has been called 'a supremacy not short of the divine right of Charles or of James.'[1] What may be said is, that constitutional law is that part of common law which deals directly with the exercise of the functions of government, sometimes securing the subject against unfair abuses of original or delegated power; sometimes protecting the ministers of government in the proper execution of their duties. The true relation.

The supreme power in this country is lodged in the people, but is exercised, as to the matter of form, through a parliament consisting of king, lords, and representatives of the commons. The main functions of government are twofold — the Legislative and the Executive. The Constitutional Powers.

Of these, the former is carried out in the main by parliament itself, although certain minor powers of legislation are delegated to the crown in council, to subordinate officers, and even to certain private corporations. The Executive function, on the other hand, is exercised entirely by delegates, under the direction of the crown, itself in this respect the delegate of parliament. It may be divided into an Administrative and a Judicial department. The latter function is evidently, in theory at least, of a merely remedial nature. Supposing the laws to be always perfectly intelligible, and always perfectly obeyed, there would be no necessity for the interference i. Legislative.
ii. Executive.
a. Administrative.
b. Judicative.

---

[1] Hearn, Government of England, p. 2.—Lord Camden reminds us, in his judgment in *Entick* v. *Carrington*, that "Serjeant Ashley was committed to the Tower in the 3rd of Charles I. by the House of Lords for only asserting in argument that there was a law of State different from the Common Law": 19 S. T. 1073.

of courts of justice. The judges are called in either to enforce obedience to the laws (more strictly, perhaps, to determine for the guidance of the Executive, whether the laws have been disobeyed); or to decide between contending parties, each, perhaps equally anxious to obey the laws when known, as to their proper interpretation.

Summary. Briefly, then, we may say that the Legislative function is the supreme power of making laws : the Administrative function is the supreme power of executing them : and the Judicative (or Judicial) function is the supreme power of interpreting them when called upon.

We may now proceed to look in cases and judicial decisions for illustrations and proofs of the constitutional limitations of these several branches of the supreme power, taking them in the order here laid down.

One caution must be borne in mind as to the use of *'Leading cases.'* the term 'Leading Cases.' The ordinary use of the expression indicates a case that settles the law upon some important question.[1] But it will be observed, with regard to these constitutional cases, that in some instances the decisions of the judges were wrong, whether through error of judgment or from servility. In some instances the legislature has interfered, and has settled the law, usually by statute; or in others the better opinion has tacitly reasserted itself. Yet these cases may be fairly called 'leading,' as being of the greatest importance in the history of the constitution. Although they cannot themselves be directly cited for the purpose, yet the whole proceedings connected with them do, in the result, establish the law on the principle involved. And the peculiar importance of constitutional law, and its intimate connexion with our national life and political development, lend a special interest and value to the record of each step in those proceedings.

[1] "Each case involves, and is usually cited to establish, some point or principle of real practical importance."—1 Smith, L. C. p. ii.

Introduction.

I. THE LEGISLATIVE FUNCTION.

i. *The Crown.*

The legislative function properly belongs to the crown in parliament, and no single branch may legislate without the concurrence of the other two. The Executive has a limited power of legislation by orders in council, &c., but only when such power has been expressly delegated by parliament.

Speaking generally, and leaving out of view such special emergencies as the Civil War or the Revolution, the only conscious attempt at independent legislation has been made by the highest branch of the legislature—the crown.

The crown has attempted to exercise a power of independent legislation in virtue of an asserted prerogative by licence and dispensation or by proclamation and ordinance: *Case of Monopolies; Case of Proclamations.* It has also claimed the right of suspending and dispensing with laws passed by parliament. *Thomas* v. *Sorrell*, and *Godden* v. *Sir Edward Hales*, were cases of particular dispensations; while the *Case of the Seven Bishops* illustrates the attempt to suspend certain penal statutes by royal proclamation. The power of taxation is constitutionally a department of the legislative power. Attempts on the part of the crown to usurp it, as seen in *Bate's case* (*the Case of Impositions*); where the King imposed a customs duty without consent of parliament; and *Rex* v. *Hampden* (*the Case of Ship Money*), where writs were issued for the collection of money without parliamentary authority.

In many of these cases the decision of the law courts was for the crown; and the true principle that the crown may not legislate nor impose, save with the consent of parliament, was not established without violent struggles.

Constitutional Law.

ii. *Parliament.*

Some of the cases noticed under this heading illustrate unconstitutional attempts by the House of Commons to usurp a legislative power in establishing rules of privilege which have led to collisions with the courts of law and with the House of Lords.

It was admitted that the House of Commons has a right to determine all matters touching the election of its own members. But the attempt to enlarge this privilege and to determine the rights of electors led, in the case of *Barnardiston* v. *Soame*, to a conflict between the House of Commons on the one side and the law courts, together with the House of Lords, on the other. The legal question in dispute was ultimately settled by statute.

Again, in the case of *Ashby* v. *White*, the House of Commons renewed its pretensions and maintained their claims so obstinately that they committed the persons who had brought actions, together with their legal advisers, as for contempt, and even summoned the judges before them to explain their conduct. These steps led to a further collision with the House of Lords, which was only put an end to by the prorogation of parliament. After which, however, the law courts had their way.

Again, in the case of *Stockdale* v. *Hansard*, a limit was set to the privilege of parliament, and it was decided that it may not authorise libellous matter to be published. Another statute was passed to provide for this difficulty. But the case is decisive of the right of the law courts to inquire into matters of parliamentary privilege.

The undoubted privileges of the two Houses, however, are very great. A member of either House is not to be called to account elsewhere for anything said or done by him in parliament; *Lord Shaftesbury's case; Rex* v.

Eliot, Hollis and Valentine; though the privilege has been held not to protect a member for what he does out of doors: *Rex* v. *Lord Abingdon* ; *Rex* v. *Creevey.*

Either House may commit for breach of its privileges : *Burdett* v. *Abbot.* Nor will a court of law inquire into the ground of such commitment : *Sheriff of Middlesex' case ; Howard* v. *Gosset.* Nor will a court of law interfere with the entire control of the House over its own proceedings : *Bradlaugh* v. *Erskine ; Bradlaugh* v. *Gosset.*

II. THE EXECUTIVE FUNCTION.

The Crown.

The crown is the head of the executive power, and as such is entitled to allegiance, the nature and limitations of which are considered in *Calvin's case.* The crown is also invested with certain high prerogatives, though they are of course subject to the law of the land.

With regard, indeed, to Colonies and Dependencies obtained by conquest, as opposed to those acquired by occupancy or settlement, the crown (subject to the paramount authority of parliament) possesses the whole authority of legislation. It is limited, however, by this restriction, that when it has once granted a legislature to such a colony it cannot afterwards exercise there any legislative power: *Campbell* v. *Hall.*

That the King can do no wrong is one of the maxims of the Constitution oftenest employed and most misunderstood. Though an action will not lie against the crown as it will against a private person, yet the subject is not without a remedy, if his rights are illegally invaded by the crown. His proper course is to proceed by Petition of Right, which he may now by statute bring in any of the superior courts in which an action might have been brought, if it had been a question between subject and subject. This mode of procedure is illustrated by the *Bankers' case ;* while *Viscount Canterbury* v. *The Attorney-General* shows that it cannot be adopted to recover compensation from the crown for damage due to the negligence of the servants of the crown. Nor can it be maintained against the crown to recover damages for a tort: *Tobin* v. *The Queen.* As the crown may not be sued directly, so its revenues may not be reached indirectly by an action against its servants: *Queen* v. *The Lords Commissioners of the Treasury.*

i. *Administrative.*

The officers of State are, as a consequence of their official position, protected by certain immunities ; while, on the other hand, the subject is protected against their misuse of the powers entrusted to them for public purposes.

To begin with the latter case, there is first and most important, as a guarantee of the liberty of the subject, the Habeas Corpus Act, the operation of which is here illustrated by *Darnel's case.* In connexion with this subject there are also given the cases of *Shanley* v. *Harvey ; Sommersett's case ; The Slave Grace ; The Le Louis ;* and *Forbes* v. *Cochrane,* to exhibit the attitude of the English law towards slavery ; and *Pigg* v. *Caley,* as the last case in which villeinage was alleged in a court of law. Finally, *Rex* v. *Broadfoot* illustrates a singular, though now obsolete, exception to the respect paid by our law to the personal right, and freedom of Englishmen in the right of Impressment.

Another valuable guarantee of the rights of the subject against the executive consists in the doctrine of the illegality of general warrants, here illustrated by *Leach* v. *Money ; Wilkes* v. *Wood ;* and *Entick* v. *Carrington.* In each of these latter cases the plaintiff recovered damages against the agent of the executive for an illegal use of power. While the Constitution thus protects the subject against the officers of the executive, it affords certain immunities to public officers. They are not answerable for the negligence or default of their subordinates: *Lane* v. *Cotton.* They are not held personally liable for contracts made by them on behalf of the public in the performance of their duties: *Macbeath* v. *Haldimand;* nor are they liable to be sued in respect of acts done in the performance of their public duties: *Gidley* v. *Lord Palmerston;* or for breach of other than statutory duties: *Grant* v. *Secretary of State for India.*

Governors of colonies are not viceroys, and their powers are limited by the express terms of their commission. They may be sued therefore either in their own courts or in the English courts: *Fabrigas* v. *Mostyn; Cameron* v. *Kyte; Hill* v. *Bigge; Phillips* v. *Eyre.* They will not be held responsible, however, for an act of State within their authority, though the Court will decide what is an act of State: *Musgrave* v. *Pulido.*

A viceroy, having a fuller delegation of royal authority, cannot be sued in his own courts for an act of State: *Tandy* v. *Lord Westmoreland; Luby* v. *Lord Wodehouse; Sullivan* v. *Earl Spencer.*

It is an important constitutional principle that only soldiers are subject to military law: *Grant* v. *Gould.* As to the relations between officers in the military and naval services, and their liability to their subordinates, they are governed by the principle that those who have voluntarily entered these services are bound by its regulations. The Courts will, generally speaking, decline to discuss essentially military or naval matters. No remedy is obtainable in a civil court for damage, even maliciously caused to his subordinates by a superior officer acting within the scope of his duties: *Sutton* v. *Johnstone; Dawkins* v. *Lord Rokeby.* Nor are officers liable to outsiders for any injury done by them while acting in discharge of their duties : *Buron* v. *Denman.* But they are liable for tortious acts done without authority : *Madrazo* v. *Willes.*

ii. *Judicative.*

The integrity and independence of our judicial system is secured in various ways. The sovereign, although he is the fountain of justice, and the judges are regarded as his delegates, cannot institute a new court of justice with a new jurisdiction, nor can he personally determine causes : *The Case of Prohibitions.* No jury is liable to be fined or otherwise punished for its finding : *Floyd* v. *Barker; Bushell's case.* The judges are made independent of the crown by being removable only on an address of both houses of parliament. They are made independent of the people by not being civilly liable for any judicial act : *Hamond* v. *Howell; Houlden* v. *Smith ; Kemp* v. *Neville ; Fray* v. *Blackburn.* This extends even to a judge acting without jurisdiction, unless he knew, or ought to have known, that he had no jurisdiction : *Calder* v. *Halket.*

The same immunity is afforded to the parties, and their advocates, and to the witnesses in all legal proceedings : *Astley* v. *Younge ; Munster* v. *Lamb ; Seaman* v. *Netherclift.*

Finally, a group of cases is presented illustrating that liberty of the press which is one of the strongest guarantees of constitutional rights. *Wason* v. *Walter* shows that parliamentary proceedings may be fully reported ; *Curry* v. *Walter* and *Usill* v. *Hales* show that this freedom covers also the reports of proceedings in courts of justice. It has been held, however, not to extend to the proceedings of public meetings : *Davison* v. *Duncan ;* though now, by a recent statute, protection has been secured to newspapers in this respect also.[1]

[1] Newspaper Libel and Registration Act, 1881 (44 Vict. c. 60).

LEADING CASES.

The Case of Monopolies. 44 *Eliz.* 1602.
11 *Rep.* 85.

This was an action by Darcy, a groom of the privy chamber to Queen Elizabeth, against Allein, a haberdasher, for making playing-cards, for the exclusive importing and making of which Darcy held a patent from the queen.

Two questions were argued at the bar : (1) Was the grant of sole making good ? (2) Was the dispensation from the stat. 3. Edw. 4, c. 4, which imposed a penalty on importing cards, good ?

It was argued for the defendant, and

Held by *Popham*, L. C. J., and the Court, that : (1) The grant was a monopoly, and therefore void as against both common law and statutes, and also as against public policy ; (2) The dispensation was also against law. The king may dispense with particular persons, but may not dispense for a private gain with an Act passed *pro bono publico*.

Judgment for the defendant.

Note.—Coke adds that 'our lord the king that now is,' in his 'Declaration,' printed in 1610, has published that 'monopolies are things against the laws of this realm.' In 1623 a statute was passed declaratory of the law, which, however, reserved the rights of corporations and of 'any companies or societies of merchants' (21 Ja. 1, c. 3, s. 9), and continued for many years the subject of controversy.

In 1683-5 the question was fully discussed in the 'Great Case of Monopolies,' or the *East India Co.* v. *Sandys*, when the grant of sole trading to the company was held good by the judges. The very elaborate judgment of *Jeffreys*, L. C. J., was separately printed in 1689, and is spoken of by Macaulay as 'able, if not conclusive.' In 1694 the company[1] obtained a further charter, upon which a resolution was carried by the House of Commons 'that all subjects of England have equal right to trade to the East Indies unless prohibited by Act of Parliament,'[2] and this has ever since been considered to be the sound doctrine.

The statute of James, of course, expressly provides that no declaration therein contained shall extend to any letters-patent, and grants of privilege to inventors for the term of fourteen years or under. In consequence of statutes of the last and present reign, this term may now be extended by the Sovereign in Council for seven[3] or even fourteen years.[4]

It was decided in the case of *Feather* v. *The Queen*, in 1865,[5] that letters patent do not preclude the crown from the use of the invention protected by the patent, even without the assent of or compensation made to the patentee.

[1] 10 S. T. 371 ; Skinner, 132, 223.
[2] 5 Parl. Hist. 828.
[3] 5 & 6 Will. 4, c. 83.
[4] 7 & 8 Vict. c. 69.
[5] 6 B. & S. 257.

The Case of Proclamations. 8 *Ja. I.*, 1610.

12 *Rep.* 74; 2 *S. T.* 723.

This arose out of the Petition of Grievances. On the 20th Sept. 1610, *Coke*, as L. C. J., was called before the Privy Council; and it was referred to him whether the king, by proclamation, might prohibit new buildings in London, or the making of starch of wheat, which had been preferred to the king by the House of Commons as grievances and against law. *Coke* asked leave to consider with his colleagues, since the questions were of great importance, and they concerned the answer of the king to the Commons. It was afterwards History.

Resolved by the two Chief Justices, Chief Baron, and Baron Altham, upon conference betwixt the Privy Council and them, that the king hath no prerogative but that which the law of the land allows him. He cannot by his proclamation change any part of the common law, statute law, or customs of the realm; nor can he create any offence by his prohibition or proclamation, for that would be to alter the law. But he may by proclamation admonish his subjects to keep the laws; and subsequent disobedience is an aggravation of the offence. Answer.

Note.—On the subject of Proclamations, see a note by *Cockburn*, L. C. J., in his charge to the Grand Jury in *Reg.* v. *Nelson and Brand*, 1867, p. 37.—Comp. the resolution of the judges to the above effect in 2 P. & M. 1554, *Dalison*, p. 20, ca. 10, where it is said "divse presidents fueront monstre hors del Excheaker al contrary, mes les Justices naver regard a eux, quod nota."

Thomas v. Sorrel. 25 *Car. II.*, 1674.

Vaughan, 330—359.

The plaintiff claimed a large sum of money from the defendant for selling wine on various occasions without a licence, contrary to stat. 12. Car. 2. The jury returned a special verdict, on the ground that they found a patent of 9 Ja. 1 incorporating the Vintners' Company, with leave to sell wine *non obstante* the stat. 7 Edw. 6.

The chief question to be argued was the validity of these letters patent; and to 'this dark learning of dispensations' *Vaughan*, C. J., applies himself.

Judgment. *Malum per se* cannot be dispensed with; and as to *mala prohibita*, those statutes only may be dispensed with which were made for the king's profit, but not where they are for the general good, or the good of a third party. He may dispense with nuisances and penal laws by which no third party has a particular cause of action. Dispensations to individuals have been numerous; the indefiniteness of the persons is no argument against extending the dispensation to corporations.

Judgment, therefore, *quod querens nil capiat*.

Note.—The law as here laid down agrees with the view of Coke: 1 Inst. 120*a*, 3 Inst. 154, 186. Blackstone observes that 'The doctrine of *non obstantes* .... abdicated Westminster Hall when King James abdicated the kingdom;' (1 Comm. 342).

Godden v. Hales. 2 *Ja. II.*, 1686.

2 *Shower*, 475; 11 *S. T.* 1165.

This was a collusive action, brought to establish the dispensing power claimed by the crown. The plaintiff sued Sir Edward Hales, who was lieutenant of the Tower, for neglecting to take the oaths of supremacy and allegiance, which he was bound to do as a military officer by the Test Act (25 Car. 2). He had been indicted and convicted at the Rochester assizes, and the present action was to recover the penalty of 500*l*. [History.]

The defendant pleaded a dispensation from the king by his letters patent under the great seal. Were this pardon and dispensation a good bar to the action? [Plea.]

Eleven judges out of twelve concurred in holding that they were.

It is a question of little difficulty. There is no law whatever but may be dispensed with by the supreme lawgiver; as the laws of God may be dispensed with by God Himself. The laws of England are the king's laws; it is his inseparable prerogative to dispense with penal laws, in particular cases and upon particular reasons; and of these reasons the king himself is sole judge. [Judgment.]

Decided :—That the king has a dispensing power.

Note.—The judgment of *Herbert*, L. C. J., proceeded upon the most extravagant ideas of prerogative. Nevertheless, it is by no means evident, in the words of Hallam, that this decision was against law.[1] The dissentient judge in this case was *Street*, and *Powell* is said to have doubted, which, judging from his doubts in the *Bishops' case*, is very probable.

[1] 3 Hallam, Const. Hist. Eng., 7th ed. 61–63.

Seven Bishops' Case. 4 *Ja. II.*, 1688.

12 *S. T.* 183; 3 *Mod.* 212; 2 *Phillips, S. T.* 259—355;
Br. 408—523.

History.

James II. had ordered by proclamation that a Declaration of Indulgence should be read by the bishops and clergy in their churches, and that the bishops should distribute the Declaration through their dioceses to be so read.

Six of the bishops met at the archbishop's palace at Lambeth and drew a petition that the king would not insist upon their distributing and reading the Declaration, 'especially because that Declaration is founded upon such a dispensing power, as hath been often declared illegal in parliament, and particularly in the years 1662 and 1672, and the beginning of your Majesty's reign.' This petition six of them presented to the king in person. Shortly afterwards they were summoned to appear before the council to answer 'matters of misdemeanour,' and were told that a criminal information for libel would be exhibited against them in the King's Bench, and were called upon to enter into their recognisances to appear. This they refused to do, insisting upon their privileges as peers; and were accordingly committed to the Tower.

Case for the crown.

On the 29th June the case came on, when they were charged with a conspiracy to diminish the royal authority, and in prosecution of this conspiracy with the writing and publishing of a certain 'false, feigned, malicious, pernicious and seditious libel.'

After much time wasted in attempts to prove the handwritings of the bishops, it was only done by calling Blathwayt, a clerk of the Privy Council, who had heard the bishops own their signatures to the king.

But the libel was charged to have been written in

Middlesex, and this could not be proved—as it had in fact been written at Lambeth, in Surrey. Accordingly Lord Sunderland was brought to prove the presentation to the king.

The document was asserted by the prosecution to be a libel, because it urged that the Declaration was based upon an illegal power.

The counsel for the defence argued :— *Defence.*

1. That the petition was a perfectly innocent petition, presented by proper persons in a proper manner. The bishops are intrusted with the general care of the church, and also by stat. 1 Eliz. c. 2 with the carrying out of that Act—the Act of Uniformity; and had a right to petition in this case.

2. As to their questioning of the dispensing power, no such power exists. The declarations of parliament sufficiently show this. In 1662, when King Charles wished to extend an indulgence to the Dissenters, it was asserted by parliament that laws of uniformity 'could not be dispensed with but by act of parliament.' In 1672, when the king had actually issued such a Declaration, upon the remonstrance of parliament he caused the said Declaration to be cancelled, and promised that it should not become a precedent. In 1685, when the king announced that he had certain officers in his army 'not qualified according to the late tests for their employments,' parliament passed an Act of Indemnity that 'the continuance of them in their employments may not be taken to be dispensing with that law without act of parliament.' Until the last king's time, the power of dispensing 'never was pretended,' on which point Somers, as junior counsel for the defence, quoted 'the great case of *Thomas* v. *Sorrel*,' to show that it was there agreed by all that there could be no suspension of an act of parliament but by the legislative power.

The two questions left to the jury were :—1. Was the *Charge.* publication proved ?—a mere question of fact. 2. Was

c

the petition libellous? *Wright*, L. C. J. and *Allybone*, J. directed them that it was; *Holloway* and *Powell*, JJ. thought that it was not.

The jury having retired and been locked up all night, the next morning delivered a verdict of *Not Guilty*.

Notes.—This trial illustrates several questions of great constitutional importance. 1. The document presented to the king might be argued to be privileged on the ground of its being a *petition*, and this raises the question of the limitation to the right of petition.[1] 2. The Crown charged the petitioners with sedition, and thence starts an inquiry into the nature of a seditious libel.[2] 3. This alleged seditious character again arises out of the denial of the dispensing power, and the principal argument both of the bar and the bench turned upon the great question of this prerogative. The last point will be found discussed in a Note; to enter upon the others would carry us too far.

Points of law on the trial.
But upon the trial there were several points of law raised by the bishops' counsel which it may be useful to summarize:[3]

1. It was argued that they should not be compelled to plead, because the return made to the writ of Habeas Corpus by the Lieutenant of the Tower did not state that they had been committed by the Privy Council as such, but by certain 'lords of the Privy Council.'

The objection was bad, since the warrant, the really important document, was sufficient in point of form.

2. Nor as lords of parliament had they been legally committed, since 'seditious libel' was not a breach of the peace, for which sureties may be demanded. But privilege of parliament holds except in the cases of 'treason, felony, and the peace,'[4] (*i.e.* breach of the peace), and this privilege secures those entitled to it against commitment.

Both these points were overruled by three judges: *Powell*, J., in each case would like to wait to consider precedents, and would give no opinion.

[1] On the history of the right to petition, see 1 May, C. H. E. 444-451; Cox, Inst. Engl. Gov. 260-265.
[2] On the controversies as to a seditious libel, Cox, Inst. Engl. Gov. 278-293; 2 May, C. H. E. 107-117, and *passim*.
[3] They will be found stated at greater length and discussed in 2 Phill. S. T. 333-355.
[4] Coke, 4th Inst. 25.

3. Counsel for the bishops claimed a right of imparlance: the crown lawyers maintained that the accused must plead *instanter*. The older practice appears to have been in favour of an imparlance; but the practice for the last twelve years had been the other way. Since the Revolution it has varied. The point, at all events, was overruled on this occasion.

4. Strong objections were taken as to the nature of the proof of handwriting offered—but these only show how unsettled was the law upon the subject of proof of handwriting. As to some, though not as to all of the bishops, evidence was offered, which would now be considered quite satisfactory in *kind*—of witnesses who had seen them write, or received letters from them, and so could testify as to identity of handwriting, and so on. The judges being divided as to the sufficiency of the proof, other evidence was required, and therefore Blathwayt was produced.

5. The last objection was that there was no sufficient proof even of publication in Middlesex. To this the Court very strangely agreed, and Lord Sunderland therefore was produced to prove the actual delivery of the document into the king's hands—which might reasonably have been inferred from the facts already in evidence.

Bate's Case (The Case of Impositions).
4 *Ja. I.*, 1606.
Lane, 22; 2 *S. T.* 371; *Br.* 247—305.

History.

An information was exhibited in the Exchequer against John Bate,[1] a Levant merchant, for refusing to pay an impost of 5*s*. per cwt. on currants ordered by letters patent from the king, in addition to a statutory poundage of 2*s*. 6*d*. per cwt. Upon this statute defendant relied, and opposed payment of the 5*s*. as illegally imposed.

Judgment.

Judgment of the four barons was unanimous *for the crown*:

1. The king's power is twofold—ordinary and absolute. The ordinary power, or common law, cannot be changed without parliament. But the king's absolute power is *salus populi*, and is not directed by the rules of common law, but varies according to the wisdom of the king. Judgment in matters of prerogative must be not according to common law, but according to exchequer precedents.

2. All customs are the effect of foreign commerce: but all commerce and foreign affairs are in the absolute power of the king. The seaports are the king's gates, which he may open or shut to whom he pleases, and he has therein absolute power.

3. If he may restrain the person by a *ne exeat* he may *à fortiori* restrain goods, and if he may restrain these absolutely he may do so *sub modo*.

4. If he may impose, he may impose what he pleases.

Petition of grievances.

While the case was pending the matter had already been taken up by the Commons, who upon presenting a

---

[1] I follow Mr. Gardiner in thus writing the name.

petition were informed by the king of the decision of the law courts in his favour. In July, 1608, a Book of Rates was published under the authority of the great seal, imposing heavy duties upon almost all mercantile commodities, to be paid to the king, his heirs and successors. When parliament again met in 1610 they debated the whole question, and were not deterred by the king's message that they were not to do so. The debate lasted four days, the principal speakers being Sir Francis Bacon and Yelverton[1] for the right of imposition, and Hakewill and Whitelocke on the other side.

The main points in the argument against the king's right to impose were:

Argument against the right.

I. Customs are *consuetudines*, and the very name shows that this "duty is a child of the common law."

II. But by the common law the duty is a thing certain not to be enhanced by the king without consent of parliament. Where the common law has made provision, the king may not impose arbitrarily.

All our kings, from Hen. III., have sought increase of customs by way of subsidy from parliament; sometimes by way of prayer and entreaty, and for a short time; sometimes even by way of loan, undertaking to repay. All which is an argument that they had no such absolute power. Even Edw. III., than whom 'there was not a stouter, a wiser, a more noble and courageous prince,' prayed his subjects for a relief for the maintenance of a war (14 Edw. 3, stat. 1, c. 21). Where merchants alone granted a subsidy on wool, the Commons complained, 27 Edw. 3, and in stat. 36 Edw. 3, c. 11, it is expressly forbidden.

From the Conquest till the reign of Mary—480 years,

---

[1] In the State Trials (ii. 477), Yelverton is said to have spoken against the right, and Whitelocke's speech is erroneously attributed to him. *Notes and Queries*, 3 Ser. ix., 382, x. 39, 111.

Constitutional Law.

there were only *six* impositions by *twenty-two* kings: and yet all these, even when borne for a short time, were complained of, and upon complaint removed. Other so-called impositions were 'dispensations or licences for money, to pass with merchandise prohibited by act of parliament to be exported.'

III. Even if the king had such power at common law, it is utterly abrogated by statutes, the chief being:—
1. Magna Carta, c. 30. 2. 25 Edw. 1, c. 7. 3. De Tallagio non concedendo[1] (cited as 34 Edw. 1, st. 4). 4. 14 Edw. 3, st. 1, c. 21.

These debates resulted in a *Petition of Grievances*[2] to the king, 1610: which not only complained of impositions in general, but also sought relief in respect of certain imposts on alehouses and sea coal: and begged 'that all impositions got without consent of parliament may be quite abolished and taken away.' A bill was introduced with this object, but dropped in the House of Lords. The impositions on sea coal and alehouses were remitted, but no further concession was made. A bill was again introduced in the parliament of 1614, but the Lords declined a conference upon the subject, and the parliament was dissolved without anything having been done.

Note.—The decision in this case was considered by Coke and Popham to have been right (see 12 Rep. 33); and it was treated by the judges in 1628 as conclusively established. For a full discussion of the whole controversy, see 2 Gardiner, Hist. Engl., 1–12, 70–1, 75–87, 236–48.

---

[1] The De Tallagio non concedendo, though recited as a statute even in the Petition of Right, and held to be so by the judges in 1637, seems to have been, as suggested by Dr. Stubbs, a mere abstract of Edward's confirmation of the Charters (Select Charters, 487).

[2] Printed more fully than in the S. T. in Petyt, *Jus Parliamentarium*, 318.

R. v. Hampden (The Case of Ship Money).
13 *Car. I.*, 1637.
3 *S. T.* 825; 2 *Rushworth*, 257; *Br.* 306-370.

King Charles issued writs for the collection of ship money to the City of London, and other maritime towns, in 1634. In 1635, having been advised by ten out of the twelve judges that when the good and safety of the whole kingdom was concerned—of which he was to be considered the sole judge—he might enforce a general payment, he addressed writs throughout the kingdom. The next year he secured the opinion of all twelve judges in his favour, and issued writs for a third time. On Hampden's refusing to pay the amount at which he was assessed, proceedings were taken against him in the Exchequer. *History.*

He demurred, and the demurrer was heard in the Court of Exchequer Chamber.

Mr. *St. John* and Mr. *Holborne* argued for Hampden.

It is conceded (1) that the law of England provides for foreign defence; and (2) lays the burthen upon all; (3), that it has made the king sole judge of dangers from abroad, and when and how the same are to be prevented; and (4), that it has given him power by writ to command the inhabitants of each county to provide shipping for the defence of the kingdom. *Argument for defendant.*

The question is only *de modo*. This must be by the forms and rules of law. As without the assistance of his judges the king applies not his laws, so without the assistance of parliament he cannot impose. Parliament is the king's court.

The law has provided for the defence of the realm both at land and sea by undoubted means: (1), by tenure of land giving service in kind and supply; (2), by prerogatives of the crown; (3), by supplies of money for the defence of the sea in times of danger. These are the ordinary settled and known ways appointed by the law. The way proposed in the writ by altering the property in the subjects' goods without their consent is unusual and extraordinary. But they may not run to extraordinary, when ordinary means will serve. The king may call parliaments when he chooses.

That parliament is the means of supply appointed for extraordinary occasions is shown both by reason and authority. The very form of the writ of summons shows that without their consent the commons are not chargeable.

A series of statutes were quoted showing the same thing. 1. Charter of Will. I.; 2. Magna Carta; 3. 25 Edw. I., c. 5; 4. *De Tallagio non concedendo*[1]; 5. 14 Edw. III., st. 2, c. 1; 6. 25 Edw. III.

There may indeed be times of sudden danger when property ceases, but this is only at times when the course of law is stopped and the courts of justice shut up. But here the time that will serve for bringing in the supplies appears by the writ, viz., seven months.

So much as to defence in general. That of the sea has nothing special. Most or all of the precedents are the charging sea-towns which are discharged of defence at land. The charge is therefore double in the one case and single in the other. Any towns not maritime ought not to be charged, which is the very case of the defendant.

Holborne, who argued also for Hampden, would not admit that the king was the proper judge of danger, except when the danger was so imminent that parliament could not be consulted.

Lyttelton, S.-G., and *Bankes*, A.-G., argued for the crown.

Judgment.　The judges gave judgments: *Weston, Crawley, Berkley, Vernon* and *Trevor* for the king; *Croke, Hut-*

[1] See note, p. 22.

ton and *Denham* for the defendant; *Bramston*, L.-C.-J., Judgment. and *Davenport* also for the defendant, but on technical grounds; *Jones* and *Finch*, C.-J., for the king.

Croke reiterated, and added somewhat to *St. John's* arguments.

The judgment of *Finch*, C.-J., may be thus summarized:

The defence of the kingdom must be at the charge of the kingdom. The sole interest and property of the sea, by our laws and policy, is in the king, and sea and land make but one kingdom, and therefore the subject is bound to the defence of both. Parliament is not the only means of defending the kingdom. The king is not bound to call it but when he pleases, and there was a king before a parliament. The law which has given the interest and sovereignty of defending and governing the kingdom to the king, also gives him power to charge his subjects for its defence, and they are bound to obey. The precedents show that though for ordinary defence they go to maritime counties only, when the danger is general they go to inland counties also. Acts of parliament to take away the royal power in the defence of his kingdom are void. 'They are void acts of parliament to bind the king not to command the subjects, their persons and their goods, and to pay their money too, for no acts of parliament make any difference.'

Seven of the judges deciding against the defendant, *judgment* was for the crown.

This decision gave much offence to the nation, and Later History. three years afterwards, in the Long Parliament, a statute (16 Car. I., c. 14) was passed declaring all the proceedings contrary to 'the laws and statutes of the realm, the rights of property, the liberty of the subject, and the Petition of Right,' and 'vacating and cancelling' the judgment.

Note I.—ON THE DISPENSING POWER.

The existence of a suspending and dispensing power as a prerogative of the crown is one of the questions which have most engaged the partisanship of historical and constitutional writers, and its true history has been consequently much debated. Writers like Lord Campbell and Lord Macaulay deny that it has ever existed; but Hallam cautiously observes that 'it was by no means evident that the decision in *Sir Edward Hales' case* was against law.'[1] An argument for its existence will be found to have been urged in a law court so recently as 1815.[2]

It is certain that the power in our earlier history was often employed; and not unfrequently with the approval of the people. It seemed indeed almost a corollary from the king's power of pardon: if he might dispense with the penal consequences of an offence when it had been committed, it seemed natural that he should be able to supersede the necessity of pardon by a previous licence to commit the action.

It is said to have been first used by Henry III. in imitation of the power of dispensation claimed by the Pope, to all of whose rights the crown claimed to succeed. It is true that even then protest appears to have been made against the introduction into the civil courts of the old ecclesiastical '*non obstante*' clause. Nevertheless instances of dispensation became numerous, and parliaments of Richard II. permit the king to exercise the power, while reserving a right to disagree thereto; and this power is amply recognized by the Commons in the reign of Henry IV.

In the reign of Henry VII. it was determined by all the judges in the Exchequer Chamber that although an act of parliament forbade any person to hold the office of sheriff for more than a year, and expressly barred the operation of a *non obstante* clause, nevertheless a grant of a shrievalty for life, if it contained such a clause, would be valid. And this case was

---

[1] 3 Const. Hist. 62.
[2] By Dr. Lushington in the *Case of Eton College*, 1815.

not only approved by Fitzherbert, by Plowden, by Coke, and by all the judges in *Calvin's case*, but it was followed in *Thomas* v. *Sorrel.*

The claim was admitted to a certain extent on the part of the Commons at a conference between the two Houses on the Petition of Right. The Declaration of Rights itself only declares that the dispensing power of the crown *as it has been exercised of late* is illegal; and when the prerogative was wholly abolished by the Bill of Rights (1 W. & M. ses. 2, c. 2, s. 13), a proviso was inserted to save all prior charters, grants, and pardons.

On the other hand the protests frequently made against its exercise were made rather against particular occasions of its use. When Charles II., wishing to employ the suspending power, issued his Declarations of Indulgence, parliament protested, and he was obliged to take them back. Of this much is made in the argument for the Seven Bishops, and Macaulay considers it a complete abandonment of the right. But no protest was made on his suspending other statutes, as for example the Navigation Act.

We may fairly sum up perhaps by saying that the power had been frequently exercised, though always subject to protest when its particular exercise was disapproved. But its legality was fully admitted by the law courts, and there was nothing in the concessions made, for example, by Charles II., to amount to an express renunciation or statutory abolition of the claim. It was the obstinate determination of James II. to employ the power as a means of undermining the constitution, that led to a new settlement of the kingdom, and the formal abolition of a prerogative of which the people had become impatient.

Barnardiston v. Soame. 26 Car. II., 1674.

Pollexfen, 470; 6 *S. T.* 1063; *Br.* 796—836.

Double return.
Soame, as sheriff of Suffolk, had made a double return for an election of knight of the shire. Thereupon the plaintiff, as one of those returned, brought an action against him for maliciously making a second return, and on a trial at bar obtained a verdict with 800*l.* damages. The judgment, after having been affirmed on motion in arrest, was taken on a writ of error into the Exchequer Chamber.

Judgment.
The sheriff, as to declaring the majority, is judge, and no action will lie against a judge for what he does judicially. But besides, a double return is a lawful means for the sheriff to perform his duty in doubtful cases. To admit this action would be against the common law, and would introduce a dangerous novelty. The sheriff is the officer of parliament, and is accountable only to them. The judgment must be reversed.

H. L.
On a fresh writ of error to the House of Lords, this reversal was affirmed.

Decided, therefore, that an action did not lie against the sheriff for making a double return.

Subsequent history.
In this case, concurrently with the proceedings at law, the question was discussed in parliament, where the election of the plaintiff was adjudged good, and the defendant committed for making the double return. After the decision of the Lords an act was passed to provide for the difficulty (7 & 8 Will. 3, c. 7, made perpetual by 12 Anne, st. 1, c. 15), making double returns actionable by the aggrieved party.

Note.—Nevill v. *Stroud,* 1659, 2 Sid. 168, was an earlier case of an action against a sheriff, or returning-officer, but, though much argued, was never decided. It was held, again, in *Prideaux* v. *Morrice*, 7 Mod. 13, that an action did not lie *at common law* against a returning-officer for making a false return. The Court also held that the judging of the right of election belongs to the House of Commons, and that it would be very inconvenient and absurd to try it in a court of law, for thus 'one might have judgment and damages against him in Westminster Hall for a matter in which he might have done his duty by a vote of the House of Commons.' This opinion was severely criticised by *Willes*, C. J., in *Wynne* v. *Middleton*, 1745: 1 Wils. 125 (in the Exch. Chamb.).

Ashby v. White and others. 2 *Anne*, 1704.

Lord Raymond, 938; 14 *S. T.* 695–888; 1 *Smith, L. C.* 264.

History.
The plaintiff in this case, being duly qualified, had tendered his vote in an election of burgesses for parliament, and this had been refused by the defendants as returning officers. Although the candidates for whom he would have voted were duly elected, the plaintiff brought an action, and laid the damages at 200*l*. He obtained a verdict, with 5*l*. damages and costs.

On motion in the Queen's Bench in arrest of judgment, on the ground that the action did not lie, judgment was given for the defendants, *Holt*, L. C. J., dissenting. Upon writ of error in the House of Lords, this was reversed on the grounds set forth by *Holt* in the court below.

Judgment.
The franchise is a benefit, and there must be a legal remedy to vindicate it. The right to vote is founded upon the elector's freehold, and matters of freehold are determinable in the king's courts. This is a proper tribunal to try the question; 'who hath a right to be in the parliament is properly cognizable there, but who hath a right to chuse is a matter settled before there is a parliament.' And again the House of Commons cannot take cognizance of particular men's complaints, nor can it give satisfaction in damages.

Decided:—That an action will lie against a returning officer for refusing the vote of a duly qualified person: and that the refusal is an injury, though it be without any special damage.

The House of Lords gave judgment in Ashby's favour on the 14th January, 1704. The Commons immediately took the matter up, and after debates lasting from the 17th to the 25th January, on this latter day they passed resolutions that the determination of the right of election of members is the proper and exclusive business of the House of Commons; that they cannot judge of the right of election without determining the right of electors; and that an action in any other court was therefore a breach of privilege. The Lords also discussed the question, and passed counter-resolutions.

Meanwhile five other 'Aylesbury men' had brought similar actions against the constables of their borough. They were thereupon committed to prison (Dec. 5) by the House of Commons for a breach of their privileges, together with their counsel and solicitors, and they failed to obtain their discharge on habeas corpus, the majority of the judges holding against Lord C. J. *Holt*, that the House of Commons were the sole judges of their own privileges. The burgesses then applied for a writ of error to take the question to the House of Lords, which is a writ of right. Nevertheless the House of Commons resolved that no writ of error lay in this case, and petitioned the queen not to grant it. The Lords now also appealed to the queen by an address, in which they show that writs of error from inferior tribunals are *ex debito justitiæ*, writs of right, and upon the queen's referring the question to the judges, ten out of twelve certified to that effect. They further complain that the resolutions of the House of Commons amount to a direct repeal of the laws protecting the liberty of the subject by means of habeas corpus, and pray that she will order the writs to issue. The reply of the queen was, that she would have granted the writs of error prayed for, but that it was necessary at once to put an end to the session, and she knew, therefore, that no further proceedings could be taken.

The prorogation of parliament left the Aylesbury men free to pursue their legal remedies, without the intervention of privilege, and they obtained verdicts and execution against the returning officer.

Note.—Apart from the important discussion of the privileges of parliament which arose out of this case, it is of importance in connection with the duties and liabilities of a returning officer. It is observed in *Tozer* v. *Child*, 1857,[1] that the report of this case in Raymond is defective in failing to show that Lord *Holt* based his judgment on the fraud and malice of the defendant. A fuller form of the judgment was published from a manuscript in 1837, and here, indeed, this point is directly dealt with. It is not quite clear, however, that this is so important an element in the case. The duty of receiving a vote is probably *ministerial*, and not judicial, and this seems rather to be the ground of *Holt's* decision. There seems to have been nothing in the case to show *express* malice; nor would this be an essential ingredient of liability if the office is purely ministerial, as *Holt* appears to have held (see *esp.* at p. 950 in Lord Raymond).[2] The later cases are indeed hardly consistent with *Ashby* v. *White* upon this view, and the attempt to reconcile them is therefore intelligible enough. In *Cullen* v. *Morris*,[3] 1819, it was held that the duties of a returning-officer were partly ministerial and partly judicial, and in *Tozer* v. *Child*, *u.s.*, churchwardens acting as returning officers in an election of vestrymen are spoken of in one of the judgments as '*quasi* judges.'

[1] 26 L. J. Q. B. 151.
[2] So in the fuller report (p. 20), "Certainly he is only a ministerial officer to execute the Queen's writ."
[3] 2 Stark. 577.

Case of Lord Shaftesbury. 29 *Car. II.*, 1677.

1 *Mod.* 144; 16 *S. T.* 1269.

Lord Shaftesbury, with two other peers, had been committed to the Tower by an order of the Lords 'during the pleasure of this House for high contempts committed upon this House.' *History.*

Some months afterwards Lord Shaftesbury was brought up in the King's Bench on a writ of *habeas corpus*, and the question of the sufficiency of the return was argued.

It was admitted that there had been many instances of commitment by each House, but the question had never been determined in a court of law.

The judges held that the return would have been held ill and uncertain in the case of an ordinary court of justice. But the Court was bound to respect the most High Court of Peers, and the return was not examinable in the King's Bench. It would be otherwise if the session was over. *Judgment.*

Held :—That the prisoner must be remanded.

In the next session this application to an inferior court was voted a breach of privilege, and Lord Shaftesbury was called upon to beg their Lordships' pardon for bringing his *habeas corpus*. This he did, and was discharged. *Later History.*

R. v. Eliot, Hollis and Valentine.
5 Car. I., 1629.

Cro. Car., 181 ; 3 S. T. 954.

History.
This was an information by the Attorney-General against Sir John Eliot, Denzil Hollis, and Benjamin Valentine, for seditious words spoken in the House of Commons, and for a tumult in the same place.

The defendants denied the jurisdiction of the court, on the ground that offences done in parliament could only be punished in parliament.

Judgment.
After arguments in which the whole question of the privilege of free speech in parliament was discussed, and the defendants relied, among other things, upon the Act passed 4 Hen. 8 in Strode's case, the judges, *Hyde*, L. C. J. *Jones*, *Whitlocke*, and *Croke*, held that an offence committed in parliament against the king or his government may be punished out of parliament, and that the Court of King's Bench had jurisdiction.

The defendants were ordered to answer, but refused, and were thereupon sentenced to pay heavy fines.

Later History.
In 1641 the Long Parliament passed a resolution that the exhibiting of this information was a breach of the privilege of parliament.

In 1667 the Commons and the Lords passed resolutions that this judgment was illegal, and also that the Act of Parliament, commonly called Strode's Act, is a general law declaratory of the ancient and necessary rights and privileges of parliament.

The Lords further ordered that the proceedings in the King's Bench should be brought before them by a writ of error, and on the 15th of April, 1668, it was ordered 'that the said judgment shall be reversed.'

Note.—Strode and others had been fined in the Stannary Court, and imprisoned in default, for having, 'with other of this House,' introduced into parliament certain bills which the tinners did not like. It was enacted,[1] on his petition, that the judgment and execution should be void, and further, that all suits, etc., against him 'and every other of the person or persons afore specified, that now be of this present Parliament or that of any Parliament hereafter shall be, for any bill, speaking, reasoning, or declaring,' were to be void. The language of the Act is sufficiently obscure to justify Hallam's conclusion that it rather appears 'not to have been intended as a public Act.'[2] This was the last instance in which the privilege of freedom of speech in parliament was questioned. By the Bill of Rights[3] it was declared 'that the freedom of speech and debates or proceedings in Parliament ought not to be impeached or questioned in any Court or place out of Parliament.' Hallam, indeed, suggests that it is not a necessary consequence from the reversal of this judgment that no action committed in Parliament is punishable in a court of law, and that the plea in the case of Eliot could not have been supported as to the imputed tumult in detaining the Speaker in the chair.

[1] 1 The Statutes Revised, 374.
[2] 1 C. H. 4 n.
[3] 1 W. & M., Sess. 2, c. 2.

Rex v. Lord Abingdon. 33 *Geo. III.*, 1793.

1 *Esp.* 226.

History.

This was an information for a libel. Lord Abingdon, in giving notice in the House of Lords of his intention to bring in a Bill to regulate the practice of attorneys, made a speech charging an attorney with improper conduct. This speech he then, at his own expense, had printed in several of the public papers.

The defendant argued in person that by the law and custom of parliament he was not punishable for anything said in parliament.

Judgment.

Lord *Kenyon*, L. C. J., held that though the court had no jurisdiction to punish anything said in parliament, and a member of parliament had a right to publish his speech, he could not make it a vehicle of slander.

The defendant was convicted and punished.

Decided:—That if a member of parliament publishes a speech delivered in parliament containing slanderous charges it is a libel, for which an information lies.

Rex v. Creevey. 53 *Geo. IV.*, 1813.

1 *M. & S.* 273.

The defendant had been tried and found guilty of publishing a libel. He was a member of parliament, and had published in a newspaper a correct report of a speech delivered by him in the House of Commons, an incorrect account of it having already appeared. The speech as published by him contained reflections on one Robert Kirkpatrick. History.

On motion for a new trial, on the ground of misdirection, Lord *Ellenborough*, L. C. J., and the Court of King's Bench, Judgment.

Held:—That if a member of parliament publishes outside the House reflections upon an individual, the occasion will not rebut the usual inference of malice.

Note.—In the case of *Rex* v. *Lord Abingdon*, it may be observed that there was actual malice, though the case was not decided on that ground; while the case of *Rex* v. *Creevey* shows that express malice is not an essential ingredient of the offence. In the absence of express malice, the question of publication would probably not now be decided in the same way. Lord Campbell, indeed, suggested that a speech published *bona fide* by a member for the information of his *constituents* would be held privileged.[1] But as it is well established that a member is elected to serve not merely for his own constituency, but for the whole kingdom, it is difficult to see why the privilege should not be held to cover any *bond fide* publication. The tendency of modern decisions has been in favour of the press, but it is not easy to understand why a newspaper owner who, after all, is only one of the general public, should have a greater privilege than a member of parliament.

[1] In *Davison* v. *Duncan*, 7 E. & B., at p. 233.

Burdett v. Abbot. 51 *Geo. III.*, 1811.

14 *East*, 1-163; 4 *Taunt.*, 401; 5 *Dow*, 165.

History. This was an action of trespass against the Speaker of the House of Commons for breaking into the plaintiff's house, and carrying him to the Tower.

Pleas. The defendant pleaded that the plaintiff and himself were members of a parliament then sitting; that it had been resolved in parliament that a letter from the plaintiff in a newspaper was a breach of its privileges, and that the Speaker should issue his warrant for the plaintiff's commitment to the Tower.

Judgment. The case was first argued on demurrer before Lord *Ellenborough*, L. C. J., and the Court of King's Bench; then affirmed on a writ of error before Sir *Jas. Mansfield*, C. J., in the Exchequer Chamber; and again affirmed in the House of Lords by Lord *Eldon*, C., and Lord *Erskine*.

Held:—That the power of either House to commit for contempt is reasonable and necessary, and well established by precedents. 2. That the execution of a process for *contempt* justified the breaking into the plaintiff's house.

Note.—Sir Erskine May points out, that the right to judge contempts and to punish them, is so essential to the functions of a legislature, that it has been repeatedly exercised in the United States. He adds, "the same power has also been exercised by colonial legislatures." But it has been held in the Privy Council that the *lex et consuetudo parliamenti* do not belong to the supreme legislative assembly of a colony, and that colonial parliaments have no right to punish by imprisonment for contempts committed within their walls. *Doyle* v. *Falconer*, 1866, L. R. 1 P. C. 328; 4 Moo. P. C., N.S., 203; or beyond them, *Kielley* v. *Carson*, 1842; 4 Moo. P. C., 63; and *Fenton* v. *Hampton*, 1858; 11 Moo. P. C. 347. Any such authority, therefore, must rest upon statute, and has in some cases been confined; see *Speaker of Legislative Assembly of Victoria* v. *Glass*, 1871; L. R. 3 P. C. 560. The power of expelling disorderly persons they possess of course, but this is not peculiar to them; as Lord Abinger, C. B., has said, "every person who administers a public duty has a right to preserve order in the place where it is administered, and to turn out any person who is found there for improper purposes."[1]

Compare the case of the *Sheriff of Middlesex, post* (p. 42) and note.

[1] *Jewison* v. *Dyson*, 1842, 9 M. & W. 540, at 586.

Stockdale v. Hansard. 2 *Vict.*, 1839.

9 *Ad. & E.* 1; *Br.* 870–959.

History.   A book published by Stockdale had been described by two inspectors of prisons in a report to the government, as 'disgusting and obscene.' This report was printed and sold by the Hansards by order of the House of Commons. The plaintiffs brought an action for libel, with 5000*l*. damages.

Plea.   The defendants pleaded that they had printed and sold the report only in pursuance of the order of the House of Commons, and that the House had resolved that the power of publishing reports and proceedings 'is an essential incident to the constitutional functions of parliament.'

Demurrer.   To which the plaintiffs demurred, that the known and established laws of the land cannot be superseded or altered by any resolution of the House of Commons.

Argument.   It was argued by the defendants, who had been directed by the House to plead to the action merely to inform the Court, that the act complained of was done in exercise of its authority, and in the legitimate use of its privileges: that the courts of law are subordinate to the Houses of Parliament, and are therefore incompetent to decide questions of parliamentary privilege. But if the Court were competent to inquire into the existence of the privilege, it could be shown to have long existed.

Judgment for the plaintiff, *per* Lord *Denman*, L. C. J.:—

Judgment.   Parliament is supreme: but neither branch of it is supreme by itself. The privilege of each House may be the privilege of the whole parliament, but it does not follow that the opinion of its privileges held by either House is correct. The privilege of committing for contempt has known limits: it is, *e.g.*, only till the close of the session. There are, in fact, many cases where the law courts have discussed questions of parliamentary privilege.

2. Nor has it been shown that the privilege of publication exists. Here the publication of the opinions referred to was not in relation to any matter before the House, and more copies were ordered to be printed than were necessary for the use of its members.

Decided:—That the House of Commons, by ordering a report to be printed, cannot legalize the publication of libellous matter.

Note.—In consequence of these proceedings, an Act, 3 & 4 Vict. c. 9, was passed, in virtue of which any person called upon to defend an action in respect of publications ordered by either House of Parliament, may bring before any court of law in which such proceeding has been commenced, a certificate from the Lord Chancellor, or the Clerk of the Parliaments, or the Speaker of the House of Commons, or the clerk of the same House, that the publication was under the authority of the House of Lords or the House of Commons, and such court or judge shall thereupon stay all such proceedings. And this is to apply also to all *bonâ fide* extracts from any paper thus printed.

Sheriff of Middlesex's Case. 3 *Vict.*, 1840.
11 *Ad. & E.* 273; *Br.* 960–966.

History. This case arose out of *Stockdale* v. *Hansard*. The sheriff of Middlesex, in pursuance of a writ from the Queen's Bench, had levied execution upon property of the Messrs. Hansard. The House of Commons committed him for contempt: and upon motion to discharge him on habeas corpus, Lord *Denman*, L. C. J., delivered judgment.

Judgment. The judgment in *Stockdale* v. *Hansard* was correct. The technical objections taken to this warrant from the Speaker are insufficient. On a motion for a habeas corpus, the return, if it discloses a sufficient answer, puts an end to the case: and I think the production of a good warrant is a sufficient answer.

Held:—That a court of law cannot inquire into the grounds of a commitment for contempt by the House of Commons.

Note.—Compare the earlier cases of *Burdett* v. *Abbot*, 1814, (*supra*, p. 38), and *R.* v. *John Cam Hobhouse* (afterwards Lord Broughton), 1820; 2 Chitty, 207. In the latter case the Court said, "The House of Commons have adjudged (as appears by the warrant) that the gentleman on the floor has been guilty of a contempt in having published a seditious libel, of which he has acknowledged himself to be the author. We cannot enquire into the form of the commitment, even supposing it is open to objection on the ground of informality."

Howard v. **Gosset.** 5 & 6 *Vict.*, 1842.

Carr. & M. 380; 10 *Q. B.* 359.

Howard had been Stockdale's attorney, and, refusing **History.** to appear before the House of Commons when summoned to be examined, was committed for contempt. It was admitted that the officers had exceeded their authority in remaining in plaintiff's house to await his return. Upon this ground he obtained damages at nisi prius.

In a second action in the Queen's Bench, he obtained judgment on the ground that the warrant did not charge any offence, nor assign any cause for the arrest.

This judgment was unanimously reversed in S. C. **Judgment.**

Held:—That the House of Commons has power to order the attendance of witnesses, and to arrest them if they refuse to appear. 2. A warrant of the House of Commons is the writ of a superior court, and, where not appearing to be in excess of jurisdiction, is valid.

Note.—In *Lines* v. *Lord Charles Russell*[1]: 1852: the plaintiff, who had been committed by a warrant of the chairman of the St. Alban's Election Committee, brought an action of trespass against the Serjeant-at-arms. By the Election Petitions Act, 1848, if any witness misbehaved in giving or refusing to give evidence before an election committee, the chairman might, by their direction, commit him. The objection was taken to the warrant that it did not state that Lines was a witness, or that he had misbehaved. *Held:* that the warrant was entitled to the same respect as that of the highest court in the country; and the jury were directed to find for the defendant. A rule for a new trial was obtained, but not proceeded with.

[1] May, Parl. Practice, 9 ed., 81; 19 L. T. 364.

Bradlaugh v. Erskine. 46 *Vict.*, 1882.

47 *L. T. Rep.* 618.

History.
This was an action by the plaintiff, who had been elected member of parliament for Northampton, against the Serjeant-at-Arms of the House of Commons for an assault in forcibly preventing the plaintiff from entering the House.

The defendant pleaded a previous order of the House that the Serjeant-at-Arms should remove the plaintiff from the House until he should engage not further to disturb its proceedings.

Argument.
The plaintiff demurred, and the demurrer was argued before *Field*, J. It was argued by the Attorney-General for the defendant that the order of the House must be held to be valid and binding, and not open to review in a court of law, as dealing with matter that had arisen within the House, which had full right to deal as it would by all matters arising within its own walls in relation to its own procedure.

Judgment.
Held:—That the defendant's plea was good.

Bradlaugh *v.* Gosset. 48 *Vict.*, 1884.

L. R. 12 *Q. B. D.* 271.

This was an action against the Serjeant-at-Arms, who had been directed by the House of Commons to remove the plaintiff from the House until he should engage not further to disturb the proceedings. The plaintiff asked to have that order declared to be void as beyond the power and jurisdiction of the House to make, and an order restraining the defendant from preventing the plaintiff from entering the House and taking the oath as a member. *History.*

The defendant demurred, and the demurrer was argued before *Coleridge,* L. C. J., *Mathew* and *Stephen,* JJ., who allowed the demurrer.

Held:—That the House of Commons is not subject to the control of the law courts in matters relating to its own internal procedure only. What is said or done within its walls cannot be inquired into elsewhere. *Judgment.*

NOTE II.—ON PRIVILEGE OF PARLIAMENT AND THE LAW COURTS.

The whole subject of the Privilege of Parliament is much too large to be treated in a short note.[1] But we must not omit to consider what is for our purpose the most interesting aspect of the subject, and one of the most difficult questions in Constitutional law, viz., the extent to which courts of law will adjudicate upon matters of privilege. The violent controversies produced by this question between the House of Commons and the Courts of Law are already indicated in the cases reported; nor is it at all impossible that similar contests may again occur.

Each House of Parliament, and therefore the House of Commons, claims to be the sole judge of its own privileges and of what constitutes a breach of them. So much the courts have always admitted—that the House of Commons possesses the authority to commit summarily for contempts which exists in every superior court of law;[2] and the courts always give a liberal construction to the warrants of such commitments, which are therefore not reversible for form. But this has not contented the House of Commons. They have not thought it sufficient to enforce their undoubted privileges, but have claimed in effect a power of legislation by asserting their exclusive right to entertain all questions connected with privilege; and have at the same time claimed that the courts of law should act ministerially only in matters of privilege, accepting or enforcing any declaration of either House. They have even denied that the judges could ascertain what is the law of privilege, as though it were a matter of inspiration vouchsafed only to themselves.[3]

The opinions of the judges in the matter have varied very much. During the last century the tendency was strong in favour of declining to decide questions of privilege in any way, and the natural result followed, that privilege was pushed to

---

[1] Cox, Inst. Eng. Gov. 85 foll., 209 foll. Sir Erskine May, P. P., 9th ed., cc. iii.-vi., 68-191.
[2] Per *Ellenborough*, C. J., in 14 East, 138, *Burdett* v. *Abbot*, and cp. Lord *Erskine* in the House of Lords on the same case, 5 Dow, at 199.
[3] Argument of Attorney-General, in *Stockdale* v. *Hansard*, 14 East, *l. c.*

an extravagant extent. The House of Commons constantly decided the subjects of common actions as matters of privilege, solely because one of the parties interested happened to be one of their own body.[1] Even in the case of *Ashby* v. *White*, however, *Holt*, L. C. J., expressly asserts the right and duty of the courts to know the law of Parliament as part of the common law of the land. And the later decisions have been much more favourable to the right of the courts to entertain questions of privilege. For this *Stockdale* v. *Hansard* is the leading authority. There Lord *Denman*, C. J., lays down that although the House of Commons has a right to declare what are and have been its privileges—it may not under cover of a declaration create any new privilege. That would be to give to the resolution of a single branch of the legislature the force of a legislative enactment. It is true that the House of Commons disclaims the power to make new privileges. But the claim they do assert will amount to the same thing, if they alone are competent to declare the extent of their privileges, and if a court of law is concluded from going behind their declaration.[2]

The present condition of the question is, according to Sir Erskine May, in the highest degree unsatisfactory. 'Assertions of privilege are made in Parliament, and denied in the courts; the officers who execute the orders of Parliament are liable to vexatious actions; and if verdicts are obtained against them, the damages and costs are paid by the Treasury. The parties who bring such actions, instead of being prevented from proceeding with them by some legal process acknowledged by the courts, can only be coerced by an unpopular exercise of privilege which does not stay the actions.'[3]

The latest discussion of the subject is to be found in the cases of *Bradlaugh* v. *Erskine*, and *Bradlaugh* v. *Gosset*.

---

[1] Denman, L. C. J., in *Stockdale* v. *Hansard*, and for some flagrant instances, see Cox, Inst., Engl. Gov., 212, *note*.

[2] The true distinction is made by Lord Clarendon, who construes the doctrine that the House of Commons are the only judges of their own privileges, to mean that they are the only judges in cases where their privileges are offended against, and not that they only can decide what are and what are not their privileges. 1 Hist. Rebellion, pp. 562-564.

[3] Parliamentary Practice, 9th ed., p. 190.

Calvin's Case. 6 *Ja. I.*, 1608.
7 *Rep.* 1 ; 2 *S. T.* 559 ; *Br.* 4–26.

History.
King James was anxious that the union of the two crowns should confer mutual naturalization upon his English and Scotch subjects; and when the English House of Commons was unwilling that this should be so, the question was raised by two actions in the name of Robert Calvin, a *postnatus* of Scotland, *i.e.*, one born after the union of the crowns. On demurrer the case was argued in the Exchequer Chamber before the *Lord*

Argument
Chancellor and twelve judges.

Allegiance is the obedience due to the sovereign; and persons born in the allegiance of the king are his natural subjects, and no aliens. The allegiance is not limited to any spot—*nullis finibus premitur*—and is due to the king in his natural capacity, rather than his politic, of which he has two, one for England, and one for Scotland. One allegiance is due by both kingdoms to one sovereign.

The point is, whether internaturalization follows that which is one and joint, or that which is several; for if the two realms were united under one law and parliament, the *postnatus* would be naturalized. As it is, the king is one; but the laws and parliament are several.

Judgment.
Held:—That the *postnati* are not aliens, and may therefore inherit land in England.

Note.—In the case of *Craw* v. *Ramsey*, 21 Car. 2, 1670,[1] the question was discussed whether naturalization in Ireland conferred naturalization in England, and the judges were divided, two for and two against.

[1] Vaugh. 274.

NOTE III.—ON ALLEGIANCE AND ALIENS.

Note.—The reasons given for the decision in *Calvin's case* were based upon the exaggerated notions of 'divine right' characteristic of the Stuarts, and of many lawyers of that time. By the Act of Union, however, which has united the two kingdoms into one, the doctrine involved has been rendered unnecessary and obsolete. Allegiance is defined by Coke to be 'a true and faithful obedience of the subject due to his sovereign.' It is correlative with protection, and so ceases when the sovereign can no longer protect his subjects.[1] It is not governed by locality, but clings to the subject wherever he is: *nemo potest exuere patriam.* And it is indefeasible—its obligation is for life. This was the earlier English doctrine as to allegiance, but it has been much modified by modern legislation. Allegiance may now be renounced or acquired; and is regulated by the Naturalization Acts of 1870 and 1872 (33 & 34 Vict. c. 14, 35 & 36 Vict. c. 39). As to aliens, stat. 7 & 8 Vict. c. 66 (now repealed by the former Act) relaxed the law. It enacted that every person born of a British mother should be capable of holding real or personal estate. Alien friends might hold every kind of personal property, except chattels real, and might hold lands for a term of years not exceeding twenty-one years, for purposes of residence or business. The *Naturalization Act*, 1870, provides that real and personal property of every description may be acquired and held by an alien in the same manner as by a natural-born British subject, and a title to real and personal property may be derived through an alien, precisely as through a natural-born British subject. It also provides for the naturalization of aliens, and enables British subjects, to become naturalized in a foreign state, and to be re-admitted to British nationality.[2]

---

[1] 'Allegiance is the tie or *ligamen* which binds the subject to the king in return for that protection which the king affords the subject.' 2 Bl. Comm. 366.

[2] Cf. Forsyth's chap. (ix.) on 'Allegiance and Aliens,' pp. 333-340; 2 May, C. H. Engl. 296-304; and L. C. J. *Cockburn's* book on 'Nationality,' 1869. The question of allegiance is discussed in *Doe* d. *Thomas* v. *Acklam*, 1824 (2 Br. C. 779), when it was held that children born in the United States of America since the recognition of independence of parents born there before it, and continuing to reside there afterwards, are aliens.

Campbell v. Hall. 15 *Geo. III.*, 1774.

Lofft, 655; *Cowp.* 204 (20 *S. T.* 239-354, *and* 1387).

History.

This was an action against the collector of customs in the island of Grenada to recover money paid as duty upon exports, on the ground that the duty had been illegally imposed.

It appeared that Grenada had been ceded by capitulation in Feb. 1762. By a proclamation in October, 1763 the crown had delegated to the governor power to legislate with the advice and consent of a council and an assembly of representatives. In July, 1764, letters patent were issued under the great seal, imposing a duty upon exports from Grenada.

The question was, whether the crown, after the proclamation of 1763, could still impose a new duty, and was argued three times upon a special verdict before Lord *Mansfield*, L. C. J., who gave judgment for the plaintiff.

Judgment.

Held:—That the crown having once delegated the power of legislation (including taxation) to a local assembly, cannot afterwards exercise the power of levying taxes there.

Bankers' Case. 2 *W. & M.*, 1690.

1 *Freeman*, 331; *Skinn.* 601; 14 *S. T.* 1; *Br.* 228-234.

Charles II. had been accommodated with loans by History. bankers on the security of public monies, and a stat. 19 Car. 2, c. 12, made the 'orders and tallies' transferable. In 1671, payment was postponed for a year, but afterwards continued. In 1677, the king granted them annuities out of the hereditary excise, which were paid till 1683. They then fell into arrear, until at the Revolution suits were begun to enforce payment. The procedure was by petition to the Barons of the Exchequer, and was then argued upon a writ of error in S. C.

The question was, (1), whether the grant of the king Argument. bound his successors, *i.e.*, could the king alienate the revenue fixed in him and his successors; (2), whether the petitioner had adopted a proper remedy.

Held :—By a majority of the judges (1) that the king Judgment. could alienate the revenues of the crown; (2) that the petitioners had adopted a proper mode of seeking remedy.

The judgment, though reversed by Lord Keeper *Somers*, was reaffirmed by the House of Lords.

Note.—No benefit was derived from the Petition of Right in this case,[1] until by 12 & 13 Will. 3, cc. 12, 15, the hereditary excise after 26 December, 1701, was ordered to be charged with an annual sum equal to interest at 3 per cent., until redeemed by repayment of one half of the principal sum.

[1] *Per* Lord *Mansfield*, L.C. J., in *Macbeath v. Haldimand*, 1 T. R. 172.

Viscount Canterbury v. The Attorney-General.
5 & 6 *Vict.*, 1842.
1 *Phillips*, 306.

History.
This was a petition of right, in which the petitioner claimed compensation from the crown for damage done to his property while Speaker of the House of Commons by the fire which in 1834 destroyed the House of Parliament. The fire had been caused, the petitioner alleged, by the negligence of the servants of the crown, who had employed too large a quantity of the old tallies from the Exchequer, and so overheated certain stoves. To the petition the Attorney-General put in a general

Argument.
demurrer. The argument turned on the meaning of the maxim 'The king can do no wrong,' which, it was maintained, covered civil torts as well as criminal acts.

The other side argued that no construction could be right which should enable the king to wrong the subject without making compensation, for the prerogatives exist for the advantage of the people. It was admitted, indeed, that for the personal negligence of the sovereign, no proceedings could have been maintained.

Judgment.
Lord Lyndhurst, C., allowed the demurrer.

Decided:—That a petition of right does not lie to recover compensation from the crown for damage due to the negligence of the servants of the crown.

Tobin v. The Queen. 27 & 28 *Vict.*, 1864.

33 *L. J.* (*C. P.*), 199; 16 *C. B. N. S.* 310.

The captain of one of her Majesty's ships had taken and destroyed an innocent vessel, as a vessel engaged in the slave-trade. The owners brought a petition of right against the crown to recover damages.

The case was argued before *Erle*, C. J., and the Court of Common Pleas.

Held:—1. That Captain Douglas was an officer of parliament, and not of her Majesty. 2. That the officer was not acting within his authority, and therefore could not make his principal liable. 3. That a petition of right cannot be maintained against the crown to recover damages for a trespass.

Note.—The words of the judgment seem to show that an action might lie against Captain Douglas, as having exceeded his authority. Comp. *Madrazo* v. *Willes; Buron* v. *Denman, post*, and the note on the 'Liability of Officers' (p. 92). The judgment in this case was approved by the Court of Queen's Bench, in *Feather* v. *The Queen*,[1] 1865, where it was held that a petition of right does not lie to recover damages for an infringement of patent rights by the crown. In *Thomas* v. *The Queen*,[2] 1874, it was decided that a petition of right lies to recover unliquidated damages for a breach of contract.

[1] 35 L. J. Q. B. 200.
[2] L. R. 10 Q. B. 31.

The Queen v. The Lords Commissioners of the Treasury. 35 *Vict.*, 1872.

L. R. 7 *Q. B.* 387.

History.

This was a rule calling upon the Lords of the Treasury to show cause why a mandamus should not issue commanding them to authorise the proper officer to pay certain sums to the treasurer of the county of Lancaster. These sums were part of the costs of certain prosecutions in the said county which are now by statute defrayed out of the Consolidated Fund, which part had been disallowed by the Treasury.

The rule was argued before *Cockburn*, L. C. J., *Blackburn, Mellor* and *Lush*, JJ.

Judgment.

Held:—That the Lords of the Treasury receive the monies granted by parliament to her Majesty as servants of the crown, that no duty is imposed upon them as between them and the persons to whom such monies are payable, and that mandamus will not lie to enforce payment of such monies.

NOTE IV.—ON REMEDIES AGAINST THE CROWN.

The ordinary modes of action are not available against the king; this is a practical corollary from the lawyer-made maxim that the king can do no wrong. But the corollary, like the maxim, is not as old as the constitution. Edward I. made 'an act of state that men should sue him by petition, but this was not agreed unto in parliament.' In 43 Edward III. it was resolved 'that all manner of actions did lie against the king as against any lord.'[1]

But the notion which set the king above the actions to which the subject is liable became established, and *Petitions of right* and *Monstrans de droit* became the only remedies for injuries proceeding from the crown and affecting the rights of property.

Where the crown was in possession of any hereditament or chattel, and the petitioner controverted the title of the crown, he set forth his claim, and the answer *soit droit fait al partie* (let right be done to the party) being endorsed thereon by the king, a commission issued to try the question as between party and party.[2] But no petition of right or other form of action can be maintained against the crown for a tort or wrong properly so called. The advice to be given by the Attorney-General was discretionary, and he was responsible only to parliament, and the crown.[3] Where the two conflicting titles appeared upon record the proceeding by *monstrans de droit* was adopted, which was to pray the judgment of the court upon the facts as established.

But the proceedings upon petitions of right have been simplified by the Petitions of Right Act, 1860 (23 & 24 Vict. c. 34), and now they may be brought in any of the superior courts of common law or equity in which an action might have been brought if it had been a question between subject and subject,

---

[1] 4 S. T. 1304.
[2] Some details as to Petitions of Right will be found in 1 Todd, Parl. Gov. 239-242.
[3] See 7 Lord Campb., Chancellors, 425 n.

and the practice in ordinary actions extends to them as far as possible.

If the subject is injured by a *grant* by the crown made to other parties, the remedy is by a writ of *scire facias*, which may be directly issued by the crown, or on the interposition of a subject by the fiat of the Attorney-General.

As the crown may not be sued directly, so too the property of the crown may not be reached by a suit against a public officer in his official capacity. The distinction made in the cases is that where a statutory duty is imposed upon any one, then, whether he be a public officer or not, mandamus will lie to enforce it. In *The King* v. *Lords of the Treasury*: 1835;[1] a mandamus was granted, as the Court took the view that the Lords were 'merely parties who have received a sum of money as trustees for an individual under the provisions of an act of parliament.' (*Per* Lord *Denman*, L. C. J.); but the authority of this case was doubted in the present case, and it was also dissented from by the Court of Appeal, *Brett*, M. R., and *Bowen*, L. J., in the recent case of *The Queen* v. *The Commissioners of Inland Revenue:* 1884.[2] As is said by *Cockburn*, L. C. J., in the present case, 'Independently of authority, I think there is no doubt whatever that we must look upon them (*i.e.*, the Lords of the [Treasury) as servants of the crown. The money is voted by parliament as a supply to the crown. .... It is true that the money is appropriated to a specific purpose, and it is true that the money can only be appropriated to the purpose so specified in the Appropriation Acts. It is also true that .... it is a supply to be got at by a certain specified process, and it is true that the crown must issue warrants or orders under the sign manual to enable the Lords Commissioners of the Treasury to have this money paid to them. But, nevertheless, when the money is paid, I can entertain no doubt that it is paid to the Lords of the Treasury as servants of the crown.' And the present M. R. says in the recent case above cited : ' The right of this prosecutor, if any, seems to me to be a right against the crown in respect of monies which are in the hands of the crown and belong to the crown. If that is so, then no action will lie, because an action will not lie against the servants of the crown.'

[1] 4 A. & E. 286 (cp. 976, 984, 999).
[2] L. R. 12 Q. B. D. 461.

Darnel's Case (Five Knights' Case). 3 *Car. I.*, 1627.

3 *S. T.* 1 ; *Br.* 162–207.

Sir Thomas Darnel was one of five knights who had *History.* been imprisoned for refusing to obey privy seals for forced loans to the king. The warrant was signed by the Attorney-General, and stated that they were 'committed by the special command of his majesty.'

The rule has been, where an insufficient cause of com- *Judgment.* mitment has been expressed, to deliver the party. But where no cause has been expressed, the prisoner has ever been remanded. *Held:*—That the return was sufficient.

The five knights accordingly remainded in prison until *Further his-* they were discharged by the king in council, 29 Jan., *tory.* 1628, the *Habeas Corpus* having been moved on Nov. 3.

When parliament met in March there was much discussion, and a conference took place between the two Houses, when Sir Dudley Digges, Littleton, Selden, and Sir E. Coke argued for the Commons.

The conference resulted in the *Petition of Right*, which insists that : 1. By Magna Carta no freeman is to be taken or imprisoned but by the lawful judgment of his peers, or by the law of the land. 2. By 28 Edw. III., no man is to be imprisoned without being brought to answer by due process of law. To this Petition the king at length assented.

Note.—The doctrines here set forth were finally vindicated by their incorporation in 1679 into the Habeas Corpus Act, 31 Car. II. c. 2, 'An Act for the better securing the Liberty of the Subject.'

Shanley v. Harvey. 2 *Geo. III.*, 1762.

2 *Eden*, 126.

History. A young lady, the owner of a negro servant called Harvey, had made him a *donatio mortis causâ*. Her administrator filed a bill against the negro and his trustees, claiming the gift as part of the deceased's estate.

Judgment. The bill was dismissed with costs by *Northington*, C. *Held:*—As soon as a man sets foot on English ground he is free. A negro may maintain an action against his master for ill-usage, and may have a *Habeas Corpus* if restrained of his liberty.

Note.—The subject of *Slavery* is perhaps strictly not a question of Constitutional Law; since personal liberty in this sense is one of those primary general rights, maintainable not against the government as such, but against all the world. Yet in deference to ordinary usage the chief cases connected with the doctrine of slavery in England are here included.

The case above is given as an earlier assertion of the English doctrine than Lord *Mansfield's* famous judgment in *Sommersett v. Stewart*, although the question is here less directly before the Court. The latter decision, while affirming the doctrine expressed by Lord *Northington*, was only extorted from Lord *Mansfield* after he had delayed judgment for three terms, and had vainly struggled to induce the parties to a compromise.

It is noticeable that only in 1729 Mr., afterwards Lord, *Talbot*, A.-G., and Mr. *Yorke*, afterwards Lord *Hardwicke*, S.-G., had given an opinion 'that a slave coming from the West Indies to Great Britain doth not become free,' and pledged themselves to the London merchants to save them harmless in the matter.[1]

[1] *Per* Lord *Stowell* in *The Slave Grace's Case*, 2 Hagg. 105.

Sommersett's Case. 2 *Geo. III.*, 1771-2.

Lofft, 1–19; 20 *S. T.* 1–82; *Br.* 65–119.

Sommersett, a Virginian slave, having been brought to History. England by his master, left his service and refused to return. His master seized him and committed him to the custody of a ship captain for the purpose of sending him abroad to be sold as a slave. The captain was ordered by writ of *Habeas Corpus* to return the body of James Sommersett with cause of detainer into the King's Bench.

Sommersett's cause was argued by Mr. Hargrave :—

1. The only kind of slavery recognized by English Argument. law is Villeinage, and the last instance of that in the Courts was 15 James I. (*Pigg* v. *Caley, q. v.*) Even here the judges had always presumed in favour of liberty, and the law recognized no villein save by blood or the villein's confession. 2. The fact that no new form of slavery has since arisen affords a presumption that the law will admit none.

Lord *Mansfield*, L. C. J., delivered judgment that the Judgment. return was insufficient. 'The state of slavery .... is so odious that nothing can be suffered to support it but positive law .... I cannot say this case is allowed or approved by the law of England, and therefore the black must be discharged.' *Decided:*—That slaves coming into England cannot be sent out of the country by any process to be there executed.

Note.—All this case expressly decided was, that a slave coming here cannot be sent away again against his will. In *Knight* v. *Wedderburn*, 1778, a Scotch case decided a few years later, Sommersett's Case was relied on, and its principle extended, to declare that the slave was not bound to serve his master here (33 Mor., Dict. Decis., 14,545).

Forbes v. Cochrane (and Cockburn). 55 *Geo. III.*,
1815.

2 Barnewell & Cresswell, 448.

History. The plaintiff was a British merchant domiciled in Spanish Florida, and held there, as it was lawful to do, a number of slaves. Thirty-eight of these deserted one night, and were found next day upon a British ship of war lying within a mile of the shore. The commander declined to give them up, and an action was therefore brought by the plaintiff against him and against his commander-in-chief, who had endorsed his conduct.

A jury found for the plaintiff subject to a special case which was heard before *Bayley*, *Holroyd*, and *Best*, JJ. and decided for the defendants.

Judgment. In an English ship of war, which may for this purpose be considered as a 'floating island,' these slaves were subject only to English law—and by that they were not slaves. The defendants did all they lawfully could to assist the plaintiff; they permitted him to endeavour to *persuade* the slaves to return.

Decided, therefore, that no action will lie against an officer who receives slaves into a British vessel and refuses to give them up.

Note.—Mr. Justice Stephen says (2 Hist. Cr. L. 55) that the judgment in this case proceeded on the ground that the ship was not in Spanish waters at the time. But it is not clear whether the ship was in Spanish or American waters, and the judgment appears rather to have proceeded on the ground that they had got "beyond the territory where the law recognizing them as slaves prevailed" (*per Holroyd*, J.).

Case of Le Louis. 57 *Geo. III.*, 1817.

2 *Dods. Adm. R.* 210–264.

A French vessel had been captured by an English cutter for being employed in the slave-trade, and had been condemned in the Vice-Admiralty Court at Sierra Leone. An appeal was brought to the English Admiralty Court.

The judgment of the Court below was reversed by Sir *William Scott* (Lord *Stowell*).

The right of search can be exercised only in time of war. It is true that with professed pirates there is no state of peace. But trading in slaves is not piracy, nor is it a crime, by the law of nations.

Note.—It is worth observing, that only a few years after this judgment, Mr. Justice Story, in the United States, held slavery to be a violation of the law of nations, in the case of *La Jeune Eugénie*.[1] The doctrine thus asserted was, however, not recognised by the Supreme Court in the later case of *The Antelope*.[2] As to what constitutes piracy, see Bernard, *Neutrality of Great Britain*, 118.

[1] 2 Mason, 90.
[2] 10 Wheaton, 211.

Case of the Slave Grace (The King v. Allan).
8 *Geo. IV.*, 1827.
2 *Hagg. Adm. R.* 94–134.

History.   Mrs. Allan, of Antigua, had brought a female slave to England in 1822, and the next year returned, taking the slave with her to Antigua. Some time afterwards the slave was seized by the Custom House at Antigua as forfeited to the king, on suggestion of having been illegally imported in 1823. The case was decided in favour of Mrs. Allan in Antigua, and an appeal was brought by the crown to the Admiralty Court in England.

Judgment.   Per Lord *Stowell.* This question turns really upon the count that the slave Grace, 'being a free subject of his majesty, was unlawfully imported as a slave from Great Britain into Antigua.'

Held:—That the slave having accompanied her mistress into England, and there taken no step to establish her freedom, upon returning voluntarily to a country where slavery was legal, reverted to the condition of a slave; and her stay in England had only put her liberty, as it were, into a sort of parenthesis.

Villeinage. 63

Pigg v. Caley. 15 *Ja. I.*, 1617.
Noy, Reports, 27.

The plaintiff brought an action of trespass against History.
Caley for stealing his horse.
The defendant pleaded that he was seised of a manor Plea.
to which the plaintiff was a villein regardant, and that
defendant and all those &c., have been seised of the
plaintiff and his ancestors.
The plaintiff replied that he was free, and the issue Verdict and
was found for him, and confirmed upon motion in arrest judgment.
of judgment.

Note.—This case of *Pigg* v. *Caley* is interesting as the last
instance in which an assertion of villeinage was made in an
English court of law.

Crouch's case in 9 & 10 Eliz.[1] is usually said to be the last,
but, as is pointed out in Mr. *Hargrave's* argument in the case
of *Sommersett*, there are four later instances to be found in print,
in 18 Eliz., 1 Jas. I., 8 Jas. I. which was never determined,
and finally that here reported in 15 Ja. I.

In the case of Crouch, Butler entered into certain lands of
W. Crouch as into lands purchased by his villein, and made
a lease of them to his servant Fleyer, who entered, and was
ejected by Crouch. Upon an action for this ejectment Crouch
pleaded not guilty, and the verdict upon the issue passed for
him against the plaintiff.

In another action of *Fleyer* v. *Crouch* it was alleged 'that
Butler and his ancestor, and all those whose estate he hath,
have been seised of Crouch and his ancestors as of villeins
regardant from time whereof memory, &c.' After a trial of the
issue and a special verdict it was found 'that the ancestors of
Butler were seised during all that time of the ancestors of
Crouch, as of villeins regardant, &c., until the first year of
Henry VII., and that Crouch was a villein regardant to the
said manor, and that no other seisin of Crouch or his ancestors

[1] Dyer, 266, pl. 11 (*Butler* v. *Crouch*); 283, pl. 32 (*Fleyer* v. *Crouch*).

was had since, but whether the said seisin of the manor aforesaid be in law a seisin of the aforesaid Crouch and his ancestors from the aforesaid first year of Henry VII., they pray the advice and discretion of the court, &c. . . . and afterwards it was resolved by all the Justices of the Bench that the plaintiff shall not recover upon this verdict, and that the prescription had failed since the 1st Henry VII.'

Many causes tended to the gradual decay and extinction of villeinage in England, such as the development of the towns, the wars carried on against France, the growing expensiveness of serf labour, and the discontent of the peasants themselves, as testified in various risings. But the cause with which we are here most specially concerned, was the discouragement of villeinage by the courts of justice. They always presumed *in favorem libertatis*, and threw the whole burden of proof upon the lord, not only in the writ *De nativo habendo*, where he was plaintiff, but also in the writ *De homine replegiando*, where the villein was plaintiff. And nonsuit of the lord in a *De nativo habendo* was a bar to another such writ, and a perpetual enfranchisement; but a nonsuit of the villein in a *De libertate probanda*, which was one of the writs for asserting the claim of liberty against the lord, was no bar to another writ of the like kind.

Manumissions were inferred from the slightest circumstances of mistake or negligence in the lord which legal refinement could strain into an acknowledgment of the villein's liberty.[1]

[1] 20 S. T. 35-47.

Impressment.

Rex v. Broadfoot. 15 *Geo. II.*, 1743.
Foster, 154; 18 *S. T.* 1323.

At the gaol delivery held at Bristol Broadfoot was indicted for the murder of Calahan, a sailor belonging to one of his Majesty's ships. The deceased had been shot by Broadfoot, while the latter was endeavouring to avoid being pressed. The men engaged in pressing were not accompanied by a commissioned officer in the terms of the press-warrant.

History.

Mr. Serjeant, afterwards J., Foster, as Recorder, directed the jury that everything the press-gang did must therefore be regarded as an illegal attempt upon the liberty of the person concerned, and told them to find the prisoner guilty of manslaughter. But 'this being a case of great expectation,' he thought it proper to deliver his opinion that—

Direction to jury.

Pressing for the sea-service is legal, provided the persons impressed are proper objects of the law, and those employed in the service are armed with a proper warrant.

Note.—The practice of impressment, though now of merely historical interest, is important in connexion with constitutional doctrines, and especially the English doctrine of personal liberty. Nor is it, perhaps, altogether impossible to imagine a revival of the practice.

Impressment of soldiers was always less used than that of sailors, and since the statute 16 Car. I. c. 28 has never been exercised except by statute, as was the case, for example, in 1706 (4 Anne, c. 10), in 1757 (30 Geo. II. c. 8), and in 1779 (19 Geo. III. c. 10, during the American war). Hallam[1] has overlooked this last statute, when he speaks of 1757 as the last occasion.

The impressment of sailors was generally regarded as a pre-

---

[1] 3 Const. Hist. 212.

rogative of the crown, though its legality was questioned by some, as, *e.g.*, by Emlyn, who, writing in 1730,[1] observes that he does not know that "the practice ever had the sanction of one judicial determination." Foster, also, could find no decision upon it, though he has no doubt as to its legality. His view was afterwards affirmed by Lord *Mansfield* in *R.* v. *Tubbs*, 1776;[2] "the power of pressing is founded upon immemorial usage;" and Lord *Kenyon* in *Ex parte Fox*, 1793;[3] "the right of pressing is founded on the common law, and extends to all seafaring men." The illegal impressment of persons not liable to be impressed was a trepass, for which damages might be recovered: *Flewster* v. *Royle*, 1808.[4]

[1] Preface to 'State Trials,' p. xxvii.
[2] Cowp. 512.
[3] 5 T. R. 276.
[4] 1 Campb. 187.

Wilkes v. **Wood.** 3 *Geo. III.*, 1763.

19 *S. T.* 1153; *Br.* 548–558.

Wood was secretary to a secretary of state, and, with History.
a constable and several king's messengers, entered into
Mr. Wilkes's house, broke open his locks, and seized his
papers. The warrant upon which this was done merely
directed the messenger 'to make strict and diligent
search for the authors, printers, and publishers of a seditious and treasonable paper, entitled *The North Briton*,
No. 45, and these or any of them having found, to apprehend and seize, together with their papers.' Wilkes
brought an action of trespass—damages, 5,000*l.* The
action was tried before *Pratt*, C. J. [Lord Camden], and a
special jury.

The judge laid it down to the jury that the doctrine Judgment.
that the power of issuing general warrants—without
names—is vested in a secretary of state, is illegal and
unconstitutional.

Verdict for the plaintiff—damages, 800*l.*

Leach v. Money. 6 *Geo. III.*, 1765.

3 *Burr.* 1692, 1742; 19 *S. T.* 1001; *Br.* 525–547.

History.

This was an action of trespass by Wilkes's printer against a king's messenger for trespass and false imprisonment. The warrant, under the hand of Lord Halifax, principal Secretary of State, required the defendant and others to search for the authors, printers, and publishers of the seditious libel entitled *The North Briton*, and to apprehend them together with their papers. He was apprehended and released after four days, as he turned out not to be the printer. The jury found for the plaintiff—400*l.* damages.

The case was argued but decided on the particular ground that the warrant had not been followed.

Argument.

Upon a bill of exceptions these warrants have been sanctioned by long custom; and a secretary of state, as a sentinel for the public peace, must have the power to issue them. As a conservator of the peace, he is protected by statute 7 Ja. 1. c. 5; 24 Geo. 2, c. 44.

Per Lord *Mansfield*, L.C.J.

Judgment.

There is no case for these uncertain warrants. Nor is it enough that the usage has been so. A usage, to grow into law, ought to be a general usage; this is but the usage of a particular office, contrary to the usage of all other justices. No degree of antiquity can give sanction to a usage bad in itself.

The warrant had not been pursued, for the person taken up was neither author, printer, nor publisher. As the justice would not be liable, the officer has no protection.

Entick *v.* Carrington. 6 *Geo. III.*, 1765.
19 *S. T.* 1030; *Br.* 558–613.

Carrington, with three other persons, king's messengers acting under a warrant from a secretary of state, had forcibly entered Entick's house, as the author of a seditious libel, and carried away his books and papers: upon which he brought an action of trespass. The jury returned a special verdict, on the ground that the defendant had acted upon a warrant from a secretary of state, based upon an information, and that it had been the custom for secretaries of state since the Revolution to issue such warrants. *[History.]*

This special verdict was twice argued, and judgment was delivered by Lord *Camden*, L.C.J., for the plaintiff.

A secretary of state is the king's private secretary, but has not in consequence the authority of a magistrate. Nor has any magistrate such a power of commitment without a power to examine upon oath. No privy councillor, as such, has a right to commit. As to the power of seizing papers, 'that is not supported by one single citation from any law book extant, and is claimed by no other magistrate in this kingdom, not even by the Lord Chief Justice of the King's Bench.' *[Judgment.]*

Decision, therefore:—'We are all of opinion that the warrant to seize and carry away the party's papers, in the case of a seditious libel, is illegal and void.'

Constitutional Law.

NOTE V. ON GENERAL WARRANTS.

The practice of issuing general warrants, in which no particular person was specified, is said to have originated with the Star Chamber. It had then been revived by the Licensing Act of Charles II., and authorised to be used by the Secretary of State. And the practice is supposed to have continued after the expiration of that Act in 1694. At all events, it had been frequently exercised even after the Revolution.

Their illegality, however, was finally settled, as well as the illegality of warrants to seize papers, by the judgments in the cases reported. Each of the cases given decides a different point: *Leach* v. *Money* that a general warrant to seize some person not named is illegal; *Wilkes* v. *Wood* decides the equal illegality of a warrant to seize the papers of a person not named; while *Entick* v. *Carrington* carries the latter point further, and establishes the illegality of a warrant to seize the papers of a person named—manifestly a sort of general warrant as regards the papers. These decisions are supported by two able judgments—of Lord *Mansfield*, in *Leach* v. *Money* in error, and of Lord *Camden* in *Entick* v. *Carrington*.

In a subsequent action against Lord Halifax, the Secretary of State, 1769,[1] tried before *Wilmot*, C. J., and a special jury, Wilkes recovered £4,000 damages, and we are told that 'the verdict was much less than the friends of the plaintiff expected, and so little to the satisfaction of the populace, that the jurymen were obliged to withdraw privately, for fear of being insulted.'

The House of Commons, while the law courts were thus engaged, was also debating the subject: and in 1766 passed resolutions declaring such warrants not only to be illegal, but if executed on the person or papers of a Member of the House to be a breach of privilege. As to this declaration, it is to be observed that Lord *Mansfield* in a speech in the House of

[1] 19 S. T. 1406-15.

Lords, objected to it on the ground that declarations of the law by either House of Parliament have no binding force, and are not necessarily to be adopted by the courts of law.

At the same time he affirms that 'general warrants are no warrants at all, because they name no one;' with which may be compared Wilkes' refusal to obey the warrant, as 'a ridiculous warrant against the whole English nation.'[1]

[1] 2 May, C. H. E. 255-262.

Lane *v.* Cotton (and Another.) 12 *Will. III.*, 1699.

1 *Salkeld*, 17 ; 1 *Ld. Raymond*, 646.

History.

Sir Robert Cotton and another were appointed postmasters-general by letters patent, with power to appoint deputies and servants. The plaintiff sued them for the loss of some exchequer bills which were stolen from a letter in the post-office.

Judgment.

The case came before *Holt*, L.C.J., and three other judges. *Holt* held that the defendants were liable, but the three other judges held that it is impossible for the Postmaster-General, who is to execute this office in such distant places at home and abroad, and at all times by so many several hands, should be able to secure everything.

Decided:—That a public officer is not liable for the negligence or defaults of his subordinates.

Note.—Lord *Raymond* says (at p. 658), that the plaintiff intended to bring a writ of error, upon which the defendants paid the money, but this appears to be very doubtful. This decision was followed in the case of *Whitfield* v. *Lord Le Despencer*, 1778; Cowp. 754, decided by Lord *Mansfield*, L.C.J., and the Court of King's Bench.

Macbeath v. **Haldimand.** 26 *Geo. III.*, 1786.

1 *T. R.* 172.

Haldimand, as governor of Quebec, had entered into certain contracts with the plaintiff to be supplied with goods for the public service. Upon the ground of their being unreasonable, only a part of his charges was paid by the Treasury, and he was left to his remedy for the rest.

History.

Hereupon he brought an action for his further claim against the defendant, and the jury, under direction, found for the latter.

Upon motion for a new trial the rule was discharged by Lord *Mansfield*, L.C.J., *Willes*, *Ashurst*, and *Buller*, JJ.

Judgment.

Held:—That the defendant is not personally liable. The goods were for the use of the crown. Great inconveniences would result from considering a governor or commander as personally responsible in such cases. For no man would accept of any office of trust under government upon such conditions.

Gidley v. Lord Palmerston. 3 *Geo. IV.*, 1822.

3 *Brodr. & B.* 275.

History. This was an action against the defendant, as secretary at war, by the executor of a war-office clerk for arrears of retired allowance, which the defendant was authorised to pay. At the trial a verdict was found for the plaintiff subject to the opinion of the Court.

The special case was argued before *Dallas*, C.J., and the Courts of Common Pleas.

Judgment. *Held:*—' That an action will not lie against a public agent for anything done by him in his public character or employment, though alleged to be, in the particular instance, a breach of such employment.'

Note.—With this and the previous case may be compared *O'Grady* v. *Cardwell*, 1872 ; 21 W. R. 340 (cp. 20 W. R. 342) ; and *Palmer* v. *Hutchinson*, 1881 ; L. R. 6 App. Cas. 619 ; *Hettihewage Siman Appu and others* v. *The Queen's Advocate (of Ceylon)*, 1884, L. R. 9 App. Cas. 571 (P. C.)

Grant v. Secretary of State for India in Council.
40 *Vict.*, 1877.

L. R. 2 *C. P. D.* 445.

The claim alleged that the plaintiff, Colonel Grant, had History. been in the service of the East India Company, and after the Indian forces had been transferred to the crown, was called upon to retire in pursuance of a general order issued by the Governor-General of India with the defendant's sanction by which unemployed officers ineligible for employment by reason of misconduct or physical or mental inefficiency, might be retired upon a pension. He was compulsorily retired, and a notification published in the *Gazette*. The publication of this notice was contended by the plaintiff to be a libel.

The case was argued upon demurrer before *Grove*, J., Judgment and it was—

Held:—(1) That the defendant could make no contract with a military officer in derogation of the crown's general power to dismiss him at pleasure; and (2) That the publication in the *Gazette* was an official act under the authority of the crown, for which the defendant was not responsible in an action of libel.

Fabrigas v. Mostyn. 15 *Geo. III.*, 1773.

Cowp. 161; 1 *Smith, L. C.*, 658.

History. This was an action in the Common Pleas against the governor of the island of Minorca for illegally imprisoning and banishing the plaintiff without trial, on the ground that the plaintiff had presented to him a petition in an improper manner. The question left to the jury was whether the plaintiff's behaviour was such as to show that he was about to stir up sedition and mutiny. They gave him 3,000*l*. damages.

Argument. The case was argued on error in the King's Bench, on the ground for the defendant, that no action would lie in England for an act committed in Minorca.

Judgment. Judgment *per* Lord *Mansfield*, L. C. J.: It is impossible there could ever exist a doubt but that a subject born in Minorca has as good a right to appeal to the king's courts of justice as one who is born within the sound of Bow bell. To repel the jurisdiction of the king's court you must show another jurisdiction; but here no other is even suggested. The governor must be tried in England, to see whether he has exercised the authority delegated to him legally and properly.

Decided:—'An action does most emphatically lie against the governor.'

Note.—It was also argued for the defendant that no action would lie against him as governor acting in a judicial capacity. To this Lord *Mansfield* assented, but pointed out that it had not been pleaded, nor was it even in evidence, that the defendant sat as judge of a court of justice. It may be noted that Minorca was a British possession from 1763 to 1782.

Cameron v. Kyte. 5 & 6 Wm. IV., 1835.
3 Knapp, P. C. C. 332.

An officer called the vendue master in the colony of Berbice was entitled to sell all property sold by public auction, and to receive a commission of 5 per cent. on the purchase money. This rate was altered by the governor in 1810 to 1½ per cent., and the local courts refused to entertain a petition from the deputy vendue master. In 1824 Charles Kyte became deputy vendue master, and, until 1829, received commission according to the former rate. Cameron had purchased an estate in this last year, and refused to pay more than 1½ per cent., and the supreme court ordered him to pay the difference. He appealed to the king in council. *History.*

Judgment was delivered by *Parke*, B. The governor might, with the consent of the Court of Policy, have reduced the rate of commission, but there was no such consent. The king, it is admitted, might have this power, but there is no special instruction in the governor's commission for this quasi-legislative act. Can it then be inferred from the nature of the office of governor? There is no authority to show that a governor can be considered as having delegation of the whole royal power in any colony; and his simple act, not expressly or implicitly authorised by his commission, is not equivalent to such an act done by the crown itself, and is consequently not valid. *Judgment.*

Judgment accordingly for the respondent.

Hill v. Bigge. 5 *Vict.*, 1841.
3 *Moo. P. C. C.* 465 ; *Br.* 623-650.

History.

An action had been brought against the governor of the island of Trinidad, Sir George Hill, in the court of civil jurisdiction there, for a debt incurred in England, and before his appointment as governor. He appeared under protest, and pleaded that he could not be sued in the said court. The plea was overruled, and the case decided against him.

Argument.

He now appealed to the Privy Council, and it was argued that he, being by the terms of his commission vested with legislative as well as executive power, was not within the jurisdiction of the courts in the colony he governed.

Judgment.

In the judgment (delivered by Lord *Brougham*). The judgment of the colonial court was affirmed, and it is pointed out that, (1) the authority of a governor is only delegated from the sovereign, and is strictly limited by the terms of his commission ; (2) The crown itself may be sued, though in a particular manner ; (3) The judges of the courts in this country are liable to be sued in their own courts.

Decided :—That an action will lie against the governor in the court of his colony.

Phillips *v.* Eyre. 30 & 31 *Vict.*, 1867.

L. R. 4 *Q. B.* 225; 6 *Q. B.* 1.

This was an action of assault and imprisonment History.
against Eyre, who was governor of Jamaica, and upon
the outbreak of a rebellion there had proclaimed martial
law, and taken various measures for the suppression of
the rebellion, in the course of which the acts were committed for which the action was now brought.

The defendant pleaded that the grievances complained Plea.
of were covered by an Act of Indemnity which had
been passed in 1866 by the Jamaica legislature, and
that the action therefore could not be maintained.

To this the plaintiff replied, (1) that the defendant was Replication.
still governor at the passing of the Act of Indemnity,
which could, therefore, only have become law by his
consent; (2) that an Act of the Jamaica legislature could
not bar his right to maintain an action in England.

The defendant demurred, and the demurrer was heard
before *Cockburn*, L. C. J., in the Queen's Bench, and then
upon error in Sc. Cam., where judgment was delivered
for the defendant by *Willes*, J.

Held :—(1) That the governor of a colony can legally Judgment.
give his consent to a bill in which he is personally
interested; (2) That the Act of a colonial legislature
must be treated in accordance with the principles of the
comity of nations.

Musgrave v. Pulido. 43 *Vict.*, 1880.

L. R. 5 *App. Cas.* 102.

History — This was an appeal to the Privy Council from the Supreme Court at Jamaica. The plaintiff had there sued the defendant for a trespass, in seizing and detaining a schooner, of which the plaintiff was charterer.

The defendant pleaded that he was governor of the island, and entitled to the privileges of that office, and that the acts complained of were done by him as governor, and as acts of state. The Supreme Court overruled the pleas, ordered the defendant to answer further, and the defendant appealed.

It was contended for the appellant, that the plea was good as a plea of privilege, and that it also disclosed a good defence to the action.

Judgment. — Judgment was delivered by Sir *Montague Smith* affirming the decision of the court below.

Held:—(1) That a governor is not privileged from being sued in the courts of his colony; (2) that it is within the province of municipal courts to determine whether any act of power done by a governor is within the limits of his authority, and therefore an act of state.

Tandy v. Earl of Westmoreland. 32 *Geo. III.*, 1792.

27 *S. T.* 1246.

This was an action brought against the Lord Lieu- History. tenant of Ireland, for what was alleged to be an act of state. The Attorney-General, before an appearance had been entered, moved the court to quash the proceedings. During the argument the Attorney-General offered, on the defendant's behalf, to enter an appearance if the plaintiff's counsel would declare that the action was not brought for an act of state.

The Court *held:* — That no action can be brought Judgment. against the Lord Lieutenant for an act of state.

The Chief Baron also *held:* —That the Lord Lieutenant, as the executive authority, cannot be sued at all.

Note.—Lord *Brougham* in *Hill* v. *Bigge* (3 Moo. P. C. C. at p. 480), refers to this case as inaccurately reported; as to which see, however, *Luby* v. *Lord Wodehouse*, 17 Ir. C. L. R. 638, at p. 639. He speaks of the dicta as exaggerated; but considering the view held by the judges in that case of the authority of a viceroy, there seems no sufficient reason for doubting that they were used.

On the question whether the Lord Lieutenant can be sued at all in his own courts, compare *Luby* v. *Lord Wodehouse* (next page), and the Note (p. 84, *post*).

Luby v. **Lord Wodehouse.** 28 *Vict.*, 1865.

17 *Ir. C. L. R.* 618–640.

History.

Luby was the proprietor of the *Irish People* newspaper, and had been himself arrested, and his office had been broken into, and his working plant, books, and papers had been carried away and detained by the police. He brought an action against the Lord Lieutenant in the Common Pleas in trespass, trover, and detinue. The Lord Lieutenant did not appear and defend the action, but the Attorney-General applied for an order to stay all proceedings.

Judgment.

Held:—That no action is maintainable against the Lord Lieutenant of Ireland in an Irish Court during his continuance in office for any act of state.

Where such an action has been brought, the court will on motion direct the writ of summons and plaint to be taken off the file without putting the Lord Lieutenant to his plea.

That the question as to whether or not the act was done by the defendant in his capacity of Lord Lieutenant is not a proper one to be submitted to a jury.

Note.—In 1 Smith's L. C., 8th ed. 1879, at p. 705, it is said that "the editors are informed that this case has been recently acted upon by the English law-officers."

Sullivan v. Earl Spencer. 35 *Vict.*, 1872.
I. R. 6 *C. L.* 173.

The Lord Lieutenant of Ireland, the defendant in this case, had suppressed a political meeting which was to have been held in the Phœnix Park, and the plaintiff brought an action for injuries alleged to have been committed by the police while preventing the holding of the meeting. A motion to stay all proceedings, and strike the defendant's name out of the summons and plaint, was heard by *Whiteside*, C. J., *O'Brien* and *Fitzgerald*, JJ., and granted. [History.]

Held:—That *Luby* v. *Wodehouse* had been rightly decided both in principle and on authority; and that the act was one done in the Lord Lieutenant's politic capacity. That case was therefore followed, and motion made to stay all proceedings. [Judgment.]

Note.—In connection with this and the preceding cases, see *O'Byrne* v. *Marquis of Hartington and Others*, 1877; Ir. R. 11 C. L. 445, which arose out of the same facts as this present case.

NOTE VI.—ON THE LIABILITY OF GOVERNORS.

It is now well settled that a colonial governor may be sued not only in this country but in the courts of his colony during his governorship. Some degree of doubt as to his liability was caused by an erroneous theory expressed by Lord *Mansfield* in *Fabrigas* v. *Mostyn*, "that the governor is in the nature of a viceroy, and that therefore locally, during his government, no civil or criminal actions will lie against him." This doubt was disposed of, however, by the cases of *Hill* v. *Bigge*, and *Cameron* v. *Kyle*, and it is now well established that a governor's authority is expressly limited to the terms of his commission, and that he does not possess general sovereign power. There is one important qualification of his liability. He cannot be held responsible in any action for any act done by him as an act of state and within his legal authority. And *Musgrave* v. *Palido* shows that it is within the province of the courts to determine whether acts alleged to be acts of state are really so.

The Lord-Lieutenant of Ireland and probably the Governor-General of India, neither of which countries is a colony, stand indeed upon a different footing, and are considered to be viceroys. It has been held that no proceedings in respect of an act of state can be even commenced against the Lord-Lieutenant of Ireland, as is shown by *Tandy* v. *Earl of Westmoreland*, *Luby* v. *Wodehouse*, and *Sullivan* v. *Earl Spencer*. It was indeed admitted in *Luby* v. *Lord Wodehouse* (at p. 627), that actions had been brought against a Lord-Lieutenant for debt in the High Courts, and that he would be liable for every personal injury or debt. On the other hand it has been held in a Canadian case, in *Harvey* v. *Lord Aylmer*, that an action of debt did not lie against the Governor-General.[1]

A governor, like other public officers, is not personally liable on contracts made by him in his official capacity; and in all cases where his actions are of a judicial nature, he shares of course in the immunity of all judges.

The *criminal* liability of a governor is expressly provided for

---

[1] Cited in *Hill* v. *Bigge*, at p. 469.

by stat. 11 & 12 Will. 3, c. 12, which enacts that all crimes committed by 'governors of plantations . . . in the plantations,' shall be tried in the Court of Queen's Bench, or by special commission. In *R.* v. *Eyre*,[1] it was decided that under this statute, in the case of a misdemeanor alleged to have been committed by an ex-governor in his colony, a magistrate within whose jurisdiction the accused had come has jurisdiction to hear the case; and if he commits on the charge, must return the depositions into the Queen's Bench.

Ex-Governor Wall[2] was tried in 1802 for murder, on the ground of his having inflicted excessive corporal punishment in the island of Goree in 1782. He was convicted and hanged, Lord Campbell thinks, 'through vengeful enthusiasm.'[3]

In 1804 General Picton[4] was tried for a misdemeanor in causing torture to be inflicted upon Luisa Calderon to compel a confession while he was governor. A question arose as to whether the Spanish law permitted torture in Trinidad at the time of its cession by Spain. Upon a second trial the jury returned a special verdict, and the court ordered the defendant's recognizances to be respited till further orders. No judgment had been pronounced when General Picton fell at Waterloo.

For an early discussion of the various questions as to a governor's liability, *Dutton*, app. v. *Howell*, resp. 1690, in the House of Lords may be consulted.[5]

[1] L. R. 3 Q. B. 487.
[2] *R.* v. *Wall*, 28 S. T. 51.
[3] Campb., 3 Lives of the Chief Justices, 149; Forsyth, *loc. cit.* 86.
[4] *R.* v. *Picton*, 30 S. T. 225.
[5] Shower, Cases in Parliament, 24. Other cases on the power, duties, and liabilities of governors will be found collected by Mr. Forsyth, in 'Cases and Opinions on Constitutional Law,' pp. 80–89.

Grant v. Sir Charles Gould. 32 *Geo. III.*, 1792.
2 *H. Bl.* 69.

History.

This case arose as an action for a prohibition to prevent the execution of a sentence passed on the plaintiff by a general court-martial. The plaintiff was charged with persuading two soldiers to desert in order to join the East India Company's service. He denied that he was a soldier, or liable to martial (meaning *military*) law, though he admitted, that for purposes of a recruiting agent he assumed the character of a serjeant, and received pay and allowances as such; or that he had been guilty of a military offence. The plaintiff having been convicted and sentenced, applied to the King's Bench for a prohibition.

Judgment.

Judgment was delivered by Lord *Loughborough*, C. J., who pointed out, that "martial law does not exist in England at all." When martial law is established, it is very different from what is inaccurately called martial law merely because it is the decision by a court-martial. The Mutiny Act has created a court to try those who are a part of the army for breaches of military duty. The only ground of prohibition by the ordinary courts, is to prevent them from exceeding their jurisdiction.

The motion was therefore refused.

Sutton v. Johnstone. 24 *Geo. III.*, 1784.
1 *T. R.* 493; *Br.* 650–712.

In this case one navy captain brought an action against another for having, as his superior officer, put him under arrest and imprisonment, and so kept him nearly three years, until he was tried by court-martial for disobedience of orders. He was acquitted; and afterwards juries twice gave verdicts for the plaintiff with substantial damages. *History.*

On motion made in arrest of judgment in the Exchequer, the question was decided in favour of the defendant. *Judgment.*

Held:—That this is not like an action of trespass, which supposes that something manifestly illegal has been done. Here it is for the ordering of a prosecution which upon the stating of it is manifestly legal.

It seems that a commander ought not to be liable to an action for exercising his discretion in ordering his subordinate to be tried by court-martial; although there is no authority either way. And in this case even if the action were maintainable in itself, judgment ought, we think, to be given for the defendant.

Note.—Point decided according to Lord *Mansfield*, C. J.,[1] that there was probable cause for the imprisonment in that case; and the reversal of judgment of Exchequer must be taken to have proceeded on that ground.

Lush, J., thinks, in *Dawkins* v. *Paulet*,[2] that this is a judgment of high authority; that every year since Acts have passed for government of army and navy without any intimation of a contrary view on the part of the legislature; the judgment stands unassailed, one which has received the tacit assent of the legislature and the profession; and *Cockburn*, L. C. J., speaks of it with equal respect in the same case, while he would apply it differently to the case then before him.

[1] In *Warden* v. *Bailey*, 4 Taunt. 89.   [2] L. R. 5 Q. B. at p. 122.

Col. Dawkins v. Lord Rokeby. 30 *Vict.*, 1866.
4 *F. & F.* 806 ; *L. R.* 8 *Q. B.* 255 ; 7 *H. L.* 744. *Cp.*
Dawkins v. *Lord Paulet, L. R.* 5 *Q. B.* 94.

History.

There were *two* actions in this matter by a military officer against his commander.

The first was an action for false imprisonment and malicious prosecution and conspiring with others to cause his removal from the army—tried in 1866.

Judgment.

Willes, J., non-suited the plaintiff on the ground that no cause of action in a civil court had been shown. The matter had been discussed and disposed of by the military authorities. Persons who enter into the military state become subject to military rule and discipline, and must abide by them.

Q. B.

The *second* was an action for libel on the ground of Lord Rokeby's evidence before the court of enquiry held into Col. Dawkins' conduct, and was tried before *Blackburn*, J., who directed the jury that the action did not lie, on the ground that the statements complained of were made by a military officer in the course of an enquiry into military matters.

Judgment.

Upon a writ of error this direction was approved by a court of ten judges—judgment being delivered by *Kelly*, L. C. B.

S. C.
Judgment.

A court of enquiry is a court duly and legally constituted, and recognised in the Articles of War and in many Acts of Parliament. And the principle is clear that no action of libel or slander lies against judges, counsel, witnesses, or parties for words spoken in the ordinary course of any proceeding before any court recognised by law.

H. L.

Upon appeal to the House of Lords (5 May, 1874) the opinion of the judges was taken, and *affirmed.*

Note.—In 1869 Col. Dawkins brought an action against Lord Paulet[1] for a report made in the course of his duty to the Adjutant-General, declaring the plaintiff to be unfit for command, &c. The plaintiff by replication alleged actual malice and *mala fides*. *Mellor* and *Lush,* JJ., held the replication bad; no action will lie against a military officer for an act done in the ordinary course of his duty, even if done maliciously or without reasonable cause. *Cockburn*, L. C. J., dissented, and held the replication good : *Sutton* v. *Johnstone* had proceeded on the ground that there was reasonable and probable cause of arrest; and in that case Lord *Mansfield* expressly said, 'there is no authority either way.' *Dawkins* v. *Rokeby* (this being of course only the earlier action of 1866) was the other way, but was a single nisi prius judgment.

Then in the *second* action against Lord Rokeby in 1873, the Court of Exchequer Chamber, after referring to the L. C. J.'s opinion, observes that 'it is satisfactory to us to feel that the general question of privilege as applied to communications between military authorities upon military subjects . . . . is yet open to final consideration before a court of the last resort.'

When the question did eventually come before the House of Lords it was settled against the view taken by *Cockburn*, L. C. J.

In *Thomas* v. *Churton*,[2] seven years before, the Lord Chief Justice had applied the same principle to the case of judges. There he says, 'I am reluctant to decide, and will not do so until the question comes before me, that if a judge abuses his judicial office by using slanderous words maliciously and without reasonable and probable cause, he is not to be liable to an action.' The law upon the question is now, however, settled beyond the reach of any but legislative interference.

[1] L. R. 5 Q. B. 94.   [2] 2 B. & S. 475 (1862).

Madrazo v. **Willes.** 1 *Geo. IV.*, 1820.

3 *B. & A.* 353.

This was an action brought against the captain of a British man-of-war by a Spanish subject for the wrongful seizure on the high seas of a ship employed by him in carrying on the African slave-trade, together with her cargo of 300 slaves. The plaintiff was not forbidden to carry on this trade by the laws of his own country.

At the direction of *Abbott*, L. C. J. [Lord *Tenterden*], the jury assessed the damages for ship and slaves separately, as the judge at first thought that damages could not be recovered in an English court for loss in the prosecution of a trade here declared unlawful.

Upon the argument of a rule to reduce the damages accordingly, the court, *Abbott*, L. C. J., *Bayley*, *Holroyd*, and *Best*, JJ., decided in favour of the plaintiff.

Held:—That the plaintiff was entitled to recover damages for seizure of the slaves, of which he was legally possessed by the laws of his own country.

Buron v. **Denman.**   11 *Vict.*, 1848.

2 *Ex.* 167.

In this case the plaintiff, who was a Spaniard, and not a subject of the Queen, was lawfully possessed of slaves on the west coast of Africa. The defendant was captain of a man-of-war, who had proceeded to the Gallinas to release two British subjects there detained as slaves. He then concluded a treaty with the native king for the abolition of the slave-trade in his country, and in execution of the treaty fired the plaintiff's premises and carried away and released his slaves.

The defendant's proceedings were afterwards approved by his government.

The case was tried at Bar before *Parke, Alderson, Rolfe,* and *Platt,* BB.

Held :—That the ratification of the defendant's act by his government made it an act of state for which no action could be maintained.

NOTE VII.—ON THE LIABILITY OF OFFICERS —MILITARY AND NAVAL.

Some degree of protection to the persons responsible for the performance of duties imposed upon them by the executive is necessary, to induce them to undertake the performance of those duties, and to secure their regular and uninterrupted working.

This protection must be twofold—first, against their own subordinates, and secondly against the general public.

1. No officer is responsible to strangers for any injury done to them in the regular discharge of his proper duties, or arising out of his pursuing the instructions of his proper superiors, or where his superiors have ratified his acts. This is illustrated by *Buron* v. *Denman* (*supra* p. 91). In *Nicholson* v. *Mouncey*,[1] a sloop of war had run down the plaintiff's vessel, while it was under the defendant's command, although at the time of the collision the ship was under the navigation of the lieutenant. The captain was held not liable, since he is not in the ordinary position of the master of a vessel, and the lieutenant was in no sense his agent. *Hodgkinson* v. *Fernie*[2] was a curious case, in which it was laid down that this immunity from action would extend to a private shipmaster acting under the commands of a naval officer.

But the officer's immunity will not extend so as to cover any tortious act which does not take place in pursuance of the proper discharge of the officer's general or special duty. This is shown in *Madrazo* v. *Willes*.[3] So it was suggested in *Tobin* v. *The Queen*, reported above, that an action might lie against Captain Douglas, who had also destroyed a supposed slaver.

2. Prompt obedience is essential to the discipline and efficiency of the services; and superior officers must often decide hastily. They must be guarded against excessive responsibility to their inferiors. It is settled, therefore, that an officer cannot be held liable in a civil court for any act done in the discharge of his duty, even though it be alleged to be

---

[1] 15 East, 384. [2] 2 C. B. N. S. 415. [3] 3 B. & Ald. 353.

done maliciously and without reasonable cause. For this *Sutton* v. *Johnstone* is the great authority. Though it did not decide expressly that no action would lie for a malicious prosecution without reasonable cause, Lord *Mansfield* and Lord *Loughborough* expressed a strong opinion to that effect; and their view has been confirmed in the later cases of *Dawkins* v. *Lord Rokeby* and *Dawkins* v. *Lord Paulet*.

It is to be observed that the services are governed by articles and regulations of their own, and the Courts will, as a general rule, refuse to enquire into purely military or naval matters. This has been definitely established in the course of the recent important case of *Dawkins* v. *Lord Rokeby*, by a decision of the House of Lords. The Articles of War prescribe rules for the 'Redress of Wrongs,' and officers must be considered to be bound by those rules.

In *Barwis* v. *Keppel*,[1] the Courts refused to entertain an action in the case of a sergeant who had been maliciously reduced to the ranks by the defendant, an officer in the Guards. The act had been done in Germany during war time, and the Court held that it had no jurisdiction—the king acting there by virtue of his prerogative.

[1] 2 Wils. 314.

Prohibitions del Roy (Case of Prohibitions).
3 *Ja. I.*, 1607.
12 *Rep.* 63.

History.

The king was informed, upon complaint made to him by Archbishop Bancroft concerning prohibitions, that he had a right to take what causes he pleased from the determination of the judges and to determine them himself.

Answer.

To which *Coke*, C. J., answered, in the presence and with the consent of all the judges of England:

That the king in his own person cannot adjudge any case, either criminal or betwixt party and party, and judgments are always given by the court:

The king may sit in the King's Bench, but the judgments are always given *per curiam;* no king after the Conquest assumed to himself to give any judgment:

The king cannot arrest any man, for the party cannot have remedy against the king.

Note.—Coke's statement that no king after the Conquest gave judgment is probably not correct, and we must remember that the 12th Part of his Reports was not published by himself. It is said in the well-known *Dialogus de Scaccario*,[1] that the king presides in person in the King's Bench, and Madox (ii., 10) mentions several cases in which Henry III. 'sat and acted in person at the Exchequer.' What James wanted was to assert a right on the part of the crown to decide questions in which two courts were brought into collision, and thus to decide that the King's Bench could not prohibit the Ecclesiastical Courts.[2]

[1] I. iv.; Stubbs, Sel. Ch. 168.
[2] See Gardiner, 2 H. E. 35, 122.

Floyd *v.* Barker. 5 *Ja. I.*, 1607.

12 *Rep.* 23 (vi. 223).

A grand jury of Anglesey had indicted one William History.
Price for murder, and he had been convicted and executed. Floyd proceeded by 'bill' in the Star Chamber against Barker, the judge of assize on the trial, and the grand jurors.

The case was heard before *Popham*, L.C.J., *Coke*, C.J., the Chief Baron, the Lord Chancellor, and all the Court of Star Chamber, and it was—

Resolved:—That when a grand inquest (*i.e.* grand Judgment. jury) indicts one of murder or felony, conspiracy doth not lie against the indictors, even where the party is acquitted.

What a judge doth as judge of record ought not to be drawn into question in this court or before any other judge.

Note.—The reason of this is said *in loco* to be that the king himself is *de jure* to deliver justice to all his subjects, and because he cannot himself do it to all persons, he delegates his power to his judges. Any cause of complaint, therefore, ought to be laid before the king himself (at p. 25). Compare the *Earl of Macclesfield* v. *Starkey*, 1684;[1] an action of scandalum magnatum against one of a grand jury for a conspiracy to make a malicious and libellous presentment.

In *The King* v. *Skinner*, 1772;[2] a justice of the peace was indicted for scandalous words to a grand jury, which was supported on the ground that the grand jury had no remedy by action, but Lord *Mansfield*, L. C. J., quashed the indictment.

[1] 10 S. T. 1349.   [2] Lofft., 55.

Bushell's Case. 22 *Car. II.,* 1670.

Vaughan, 135; 6 *S. T.* 999; 6 *Br.* 120–144.

History. A jury had acquitted William Penn and William Mead at the Old Bailey Sessions, on a charge of preaching in a London street, and had been fined by the Recorder forty marks each for contempt in doing so, and in default committed. A habeas corpus was moved, and the return was that the prisoners had been committed for finding 'contra plenam et manifestam evidentiam, et contra directionem curiæ in materia legis.'

Judgment. Per *Vaughan,* C. J.: The return is insufficient, for it gives the Court no opportunity of forming their own judgment as to the sufficiency of the evidence. Nor is the Court bound to accept the opinion of the sessions court, for judges' decisions are constantly reversed. Then (1) the jury may have evidence before them that the judge has not; (2) in any case they do not find the law, and therefore cannot return a verdict contra directionem curiæ in materia legis. Without a previous knowledge of the facts the judge cannot direct, and he only knows the facts from the determination of the jury. They should be said to have acquitted against the evidence, corruptly and knowing the evidence to be full and manifest.

Decided:—That finding against the evidence, or direction of the court, is no sufficient cause to fine a jury.

Hamond v. Howell. 26 *Car. II.*, 1675.

2 *Mod.* 218 (*cp.* 1 *Mod.* 184).

The plaintiff had been one of the jury on the trial of Penn and Mead,[1] and had been committed. He now brought an action of false imprisonment against the Recorder of London (the defendant), the Mayor and the whole court at the Old Bailey.

The case was argued before *Vaughan*, C.J., and the Court of Common Pleas. But the whole Court were of opinion 'that the bringing of this action was a greater offence than the fining of the plaintiff and committing him for non-payment; the court had jurisdiction of the cause... they thought it to be a misdemeanor in the jury to acquit the prisoners, which in truth was not so, and therefore it was an error in their judgments, for which no action will lie.'

Held :—That an action will not lie against a judge for what he doth judicially though erroneously.

History.

Judgment.

---

[1] Cp. *Bushell's case*, opposite.

Houlden v. Smith. 13 *Vict.*, 1850.

14 *Q. B.* 841.

History.

This was an action of trespass for false imprisonment. The defendant, as county court judge, had ordered the plaintiff to be committed for contempt in not appearing before him upon a summons. The plaintiff did not reside in the county court district of which the defendant was judge, but in a neighbouring district, and this was known to the defendant, who supposed, nevertheless, that he had authority.

Judgment.

Held :—That the commitment being in excess of jurisdiction, and made under a mistake in the law and not of the facts, the judge was liable in trespass.

Note.—In *Scott* v. *Stansfield*, 1868 ; L. R. 3 Exch. 220, the defendant was also a county court judge. The defendant in his capacity as judge, and while sitting in his court, had said of the plaintiff, an accountant, that he was "a harpy preying on the vitals of the poor." The plaintiff brought an action of slander, but upon demurrer it was—

Held:—That "no such action would lie, even where the words used by the judge were alleged to have been spoken maliciously and without probable cause, and to have been irrelevant to the matter before him." (*Per Kelly*, C. B., at p. 222.)

Kemp v. Neville. 24 *Vict.*, 1861.

10 *C. B. N. S.* 523 ; *Br.* 734.

The plaintiff, a milliner, had been arrested in the company of several undergraduates at Cambridge, and had been committed to prison for fourteen days as a person of bad character, by the defendant, the vice-chancellor of the University, in the course of his judicial duties. She recovered damages against him in an action for assault and false imprisonment. The defendant moved to enter the verdict for himself. *History.*

The plaintiff relied mainly on certain minor points arising out of the peculiar administration of the proctorial system at Cambridge, which rests upon a charter of Elizabeth, confirmed by statute 13 Eliz. c. 19. (1.) No witnesses were examined on oath at the hearing by the vice-chancellor, nor were certain persons sent for to whom she referred as to her character. (2.) There was no warrant in writing. (3.) The place of imprisonment (called the spinning-house) was unlawful, not being a common gaol. *Argument.*

These were overruled on the ground (1, 2) that the charter prescribed no particular procedure ; (3) that as to the place of confinement, the court was bound to suppose in favour of the existing user. *Judgment.*

But the main contention of the defendant was that as he acted throughout to the best of his judgment in his judicial capacity as judge of a court of record, no action of trespass could lie for anything done by him as judge ; and in that he was right.

Fray v. Blackburn. 26 Vict., 1863.

3 Best & Smith, 576.

History. The plaintiff had been plaintiff in a previous action heard before Sir *Colin Blackburn*, one of the judges of the Queen's Bench, and had obtained a rule nisi, which the defendant at the hearing refused to make absolute. She now brought an action against him, and claimed 50*l*. damages.

Demurrer. The defendant demurred ' that no action lies against a judge of a superior court for anything done by him in his judicial capacity ; (2) that the declaration was bad for not alleging malice and want of reasonable and probable cause.'

Argument. The plaintiff argued her own case, and was refused leave to amend, because, though it be alleged that the act charged was done maliciously and corruptly, that will not make the declaration good.

Judgment. *Decided*:—That an action does not lie against a judge of one of the superior courts for a judicial act, though it be alleged to have been done maliciously and corruptly.

Calder v. **Halket.**   2 *Vict.*, 1839.

3 *Moo. P. C. C.* 28.

This was a case before the Privy Council, on appeal *History.*
from the Supreme Court of Judicature at Fort William,
in Bengal. The plaintiff had been apprehended, by
order of the defendant—who was a magistrate having
jurisdiction over Asiatics only, and the plaintiff was a
European—for supposed participation in a riot. He
brought an action for assault and false imprisonment,
and upon a verdict being entered for the defendant, the
plaintiff appealed. By statute (21 Geo. 3, c. 70, s. 24),
the provincial magistrates in India have the same immunity from actions extended to them in respect of
their judicial functions, as judges have in this country.

It was argued for the appellant that as the act in *Argument.*
question was in excess of his jurisdiction, which extended only to natives, an action would lie.

Judgment was given by *Parke*, B., and it was held *Judgment.*
that the plaintiff was bound to show that the judge knew,
or ought to have known, the defect of jurisdiction, but of
this there was no evidence, and the appeal must be
dismissed.

Decided :—That a judge is not liable in trespass for a
judicial act, without jurisdiction, unless he knew or
ought to have known of the defect, and it lies on the
plaintiff in every such case to prove that fact.

NOTE VIII.—ON THE LIABILITY OF JUDGES.

The law as to the civil and criminal irresponsibility of judges is well settled. No judge is liable to any proceedings before any ordinary tribunal for any judicial act or omission—with two singular exceptions, the refusal of a writ of habeas corpus in vacation, expressly provided for in the Act,[1] or the refusal of a bill of exceptions.[2] 'A series of decisions from the time of Coke (in *Floyd* v. *Barker*) to *Fray* v. *Blackburn*, established that no action will lie against a judge for acts done or words spoken in his judicial capacity in a court of justice.'[3] And judicial acts are not only those done in open court, but all those emanating from the legal duties of a judge, as for example, acts done in chambers.[4]

This doctrine has been applied not only to the superior courts, but to the court of a coroner, and to a court-martial, which are not courts of record. And it does not matter although malice and corruption be alleged, or want of reasonable and probable cause. Nor even if the judge exceeds his jurisdiction will he be liable to an action, unless the plaintiff can prove that he knew, or ought to have known, the defect of jurisdiction.

This rule has been established to secure the independence of the judges and to maintain their authority. For this purpose they must be free from the liability to harassing and vexatious actions at the suit of discontented parties.

The decisions cover the cases of the highest judge in the land, the Lord Chancellor, the Superior Courts, the court of the Vice-Chancellor of a University, an ecclesiastical judge, a coroner, and a county court judge; nay, it has even been extended by analogy to the case of an arbitrator or referee.[5]

Magistrates or justices of the peace are not protected to the same extent. Their case is specially provided for by 11 & 12 Vict. cc. 42—44 (Jervis's Acts), and an action will lie against them in either of two events :

[1] By 31 Car. 2, c. 2, s. 9.
[2] By Stat. Westm. 2, 13 Edw. 1, c. 31.
[3] *Per Kelly*, C. B., in *Scott* v. *Stansfield*, L. R. 3 Ex. 223.
[4] *Taaf* v. *Downes*, 3 Moo. P. C. C. 60.
[5] *Pappa* v. *Rose*, L. R. 7 C. P. 525 (Ex. Ch.)

1. For an act done without their jurisdiction.
2. For an act done within their jurisdiction, but maliciously and without probable cause.

What remedies then are provided in case of error or misconduct on the part of judges?

For errors in law a remedy exists in an elaborate system of appeals. For actual misconduct in the case of judges of the superior courts, the constitutional remedies are by impeachment, or by removal on the address of both Houses of Parliament. Since the Revolution there has been only one instance of such impeachment—the case of Lord Chancellor *Macclesfield* in 1725; though there have been several cases in which parliamentary proceedings have been taken, in one of which a judge has been removed from office.[1]

The judges of inferior courts, however, are subject to the control of the Queen's Bench, and are removable for misbehaviour at common law or by statute. The Lord Chancellor may remove a coroner or a county court judge for inability or misconduct.

A justice of the peace is subject to a criminal information for misbehaviour, and may be discharged from the commission at the pleasure of the crown.

[1] Until the Act of Settlement (12 & 13 Will. 3, c. 2) the judges were of course removable at the pleasure of the crown. By that Act it was enacted that their commissions should remain in force notwithstanding the demise of the crown, provided that the crown might remove them "upon the address of both Houses of Parliament." The first case in which such an address was proposed was that of Mr. Justice *Fox* (an Irish judge) in 1805. In 1828 Sir *Jonah Barrington* was, on an address, removed from the office of Admiralty judge in Ireland. Abortive and unfounded proceedings were taken in the House of Commons in the cases of Lord *Abinger* (1843) and Sir *Fitzroy Kelly* (1867). The control exercised by Parliament over the judicial system will be found fully treated in 2 Todd, Parl. Gov., 724-766 (c. vi.).

Astley v. Younge. 32 *Geo. III.*, 1759.
2 *Burr.* 807.

History.

This was an action of slander. The defendant was a justice of the peace, and had refused to grant a licence for a public inn. An application was then made to the Court of King's Bench concerning the refusal, and on this application the plaintiff made an affidavit in reference thereto. The defendant answered this affidavit by another, in which he alleged the plaintiff's affidavit to have been 'falsely sworn.'

The plaintiff thereupon brought his action, and the defendant demurred. The demurrer was argued before Lord *Mansfield*, L. C. J., and the court, who 'unanimously and clearly'—

Judgment.

Held:—That no action would lie against the defendant for words 'only spoken in his own defence, and by way of justification in law, and in a legal and judicial way.'

Note.—The immunity of the parties to legal proceedings may no doubt be put on the ground of privilege arising from interest, and this might be extended to advocates, who are only the mouthpieces of the parties. It would be more difficult to extend it so as to cover the case of witnesses, at all events, so far as the immunity has been caused in such a case as *Seaman* v. *Netherclift* (see p. 106, *post*). It seems more satisfactory to put the immunity in all these cases upon the ground that parties and witnesses alike, when once legal proceedings have been commenced, are engaged, as it were, in the discharge of a public function, the proper performance of which is by this means more effectually secured.

Munster *v.* Lamb.   46 *Vict.*, 1883.
L. R. 11 *Q. B. D.* 588.

This was an action by the plaintiff against a   History.
solicitor for words spoken of the plaintiff by the defendant while he was defending a client in a judicial tribunal. The defamatory suggestion made by the defendant was unsupported by any evidence in the case.

At the trial the plaintiff was nonsuited by *Williams,* J. The divisional court refused to grant a new trial, and the plaintiff appealed.

The Court of Appeal, *Brett*, M. R., and *Fry*, L. J.,

Held :—That no action will lie against an advocate   Judgment.
for words spoken in a judicial proceeding, though they are spoken maliciously and without excuse, and are wholly irrelevant.

Seaman *v.* Netherclift. 40 *Vict.*, 1876.

L. R. 2 *C. P. D.* 53 (*cp.* 1 *C. P. D.* 540).

History.   This was an action of slander. The defendant, an expert in handwriting, had given evidence in a suit to establish a will in which he pronounced the signature to the will, of which the plaintiff was an attesting witness, to be a forgery. The genuineness of the signature was established, and the judge made some observations on the defendant's presumption. Afterwards, in another proceeding on a charge of forgery, he was asked, in cross-examination, as to the observations of the judge above mentioned. He answered the question, and added that he believed 'that will to be a rank forgery.' The plaintiff then brought the present action.

It was tried before *Coleridge,* C. J., and a verdict found for the plaintiff. On motion to enter judgment for the defendant, *Coleridge,* C. J., and *Brett,* J., decided in favour of the defendant.

The case went to the Court of Appeal (*Cockburn,* L. C. J., *Bramwell* and *Amphlett,* JJ.A.), which

Judgment.   *Held:*—That words spoken by a witness in the course of and having reference to a judicial enquiry are absolutely privileged.

Note.—Perhaps the earliest instance of an action against a witness was *Damport* v. *Sympson,* 1597 ; when a disappointed plaintiff sued one of his opponent's witnesses for perjury, and recovered a verdict and damages. But it was held upon motion in arrest of judgment that ' action lay not.'

It may be noted how the principle of privilege in these cases has been gradually developed. In *Hodgson* v. *Scarlett,* 1818; 1 B. & A. 232, it was decided, following *Brook* v. *Montague,* 1606 ; Cro., James, 90, that an advocate's privilege only protects him so long as what he says is relevant ; and *Coleridge,*

Liability of Witnesses.

L. C. J., points out in *Seaman* v. *Netherclift*[1] that 'it has never yet been decided that they would not be subject to an action for words spoken even during the conduct of a case, if the words were irrelevant, *mala fide*, and spoken with express malice.'

Of course *Munster* v. *Lamb* has now decided this very point, and in the same way, though the present case only covers expressly words spoken by a witness relevant to the inquiry, it may perhaps be assumed, with the utmost respect for Lord *Bramwell's* dictum in *Seaman* v. *Netherclift*,[2] that the privilege of a witness would, if the case arose, be held to extend quite as far as that of an advocate.

It was held in *Goffin* v. *Donnelly*, 1881; L. R. 6 Q. B.,D. 307, that the privilege extends to the case of a witness giving evidence before a Select Committee of the House of Commons.

It may be worth noticing that, although a witness is protected in respect of anything he says in giving evidence, he is liable to an action if he fails to attend upon the subpœna of the party summoning him.

[1] 1 C. P. D. at 545.
[2] 2 C. P. D. at p. 60.

Wason v. **Walter.** 32 *Vict.*, 1868.

L. R. 4 *Q. B.* 73.

History.
This was an action of libel against one of the proprietors of the *Times* newspaper, for a report of a debate in the House of Lords, in which statements had been made reflecting on the plaintiff.

There was another count in respect of a leading article on the debate.

The action was tried before *Cockburn*, L. C. J., who directed the jury, that if the matter charged as a libel was an accurate report of the debate, the occasion was privileged, and that as to the second count a public writer is entitled to make fair and reasonable comments on matters of public interest.

The jury found for the defendant. A rule having been obtained for a new trial, was argued and the judgment of the court delivered by *Cockburn*, L. C. J.

Judgment.
Held:—That a faithful report in a public newspaper of a debate in parliament is not actionable at the suit of a person whose character may have been called in question in the debate.

Curry v. Walter. 36 *Geo. III.*, 1796.

1 *Bos. & P.* 525.

This was an action for publishing a libel on the plaintiff in the *Times*. The libel purported to be an account of an application to the King's Bench for an information against the plaintiff and another, both justices of the peace, for refusing to license an inn. The ground of the application was, that there was a conspiracy between the justices and the innkeeper's landlord to find a pretence for refusing the licence. *History.*

The case was tried by *Eyre*, C. J., and a jury, the C. J. directing them that though the matter contained in the paper might be very injurious to the character of the magistrates, yet, being a true account of what took place in a court of justice, which is open to all the world, the publication was not unlawful. The jury found a verdict for the defendant. *Verdict.*

A rule was obtained for a new trial, when the Court (*Eyre*, C. J., *Buller, Heath, Rooke*, JJ.) *Judgment.*

Held:—That this action could not be maintained.[1]

[1] The case stood over on another point, and no judgment was ever given.

Usill v. Hales. 41 *Vict.*, 1878.

L. R. 3 *C. P. D.* 319.

History. This was an action against the publisher for an alleged libel published in the *Daily News*, consisting of a report of an application made by three persons to a police magistrate for a summons against the plaintiff. The application was *ex parte*, and the magistrate held that it was a matter of contract, and not a case for criminal process, and referred them to the county court.

The action was tried before *Cockburn*, L. C. J., who directed the jury that the publication, if a fair and impartial report, was privileged.

It was argued on a rule nisi for a new trial, and it was by *Coleridge*, L. C. J., and *Lopes*, J.,

Judgment. *Decided*:—That a fair and impartial report of a proceeding in a police court, even though it was an *ex parte* and preliminary proceeding, is privileged.

Note.—Compare the case of *Lewis* v. *Levy*, 1858; E. B. & E. 537, nearly to the same effect. There, however, the reporter had expressed an opinion, and this was held not to be privileged, and Lord *Campbell*, L.C.J., said, 'we are not prepared to lay down for law that the publication of preliminary inquiries before magistrates is universally lawful; but we are not prepared to lay down for law that the publication of such inquiries is universally unlawful.'

Davison *v.* Duncan.   20 *Vict.*, 1857.

7 *E. & B.* 229.

This was an action for a libel contained in the report of the proceedings at a meeting of Improvement Commissioners to which the public were admitted. The defendant demurred, alleging that it was a true account published without malice. *History.*

The demurrer was heard before *Campbell*, L. C. J., *Coleridge, Wightman,* and *Crompton,* JJ., and allowed.

Decided:—That it has never yet been held that privilege extends to a report of what takes place at all public meetings. *Judgment.*

Note.—In 1858 Lord *Campbell* brought in a bill to make reports of certain public meetings privileged, which was however thrown out. In the debate it was assumed by all the law lords that the principle is here correctly laid down. This case was also followed in *Purcell* v. *Sowler*, 1877 ; L. R. 2 C. P. D. 215 (C. A.). Now see the Newspaper Libel and Registration Act, 1881 (44 & 45 Vict. c. 60), which enacts that :—

(S. 2.) " Any report published in any newspaper of the proceedings of a public meeting shall be privileged, if such meeting was lawfully convened for a lawful purpose and open to the public, and if such report was fair and accurate and published without malice, and if the publication of the matter complained of was for the public benefit."

(S. 3.) " No criminal prosecution shall be commenced against any proprietor, publisher, editor, or any person responsible for the publication of a newspaper for any libel published therein, without the written fiat or allowance of the Director of Public Prosecutions in England or Her Majesty's Attorney-General in Ireland being first had and obtained."

APPENDIX.

Attorney-General *v.* Bradlaugh. 48 *Vict.*, 1884.

(Not yet reported; See TIMES, *June* 30, *Dec.* 8, 1884, *and Jan.* 29, 1885.)

THIS was an information by the Attorney-General to recover a penalty from the defendant for sitting and voting as a member of the House of Commons, on the 11th of February, 1884, without having taken the oath in the manner required by the Parliamentary Oaths Act 1866. In view of the importance of the point involved, the trial was at Bar before *Coleridge*, L.C.J., *Grove*, J., and *Huddleston*, B.

The *Lord Chief Justice*, in summing up the case to the jury, said that the two main questions for them were: 1st. Did the defendant take the oath within the meaning of the Act; 2nd. Was he a person capable in law of taking the oath in the sense of the Act? Some minor questions were also put to the jury.

The jury found, 1st, that the defendant when he took the oath on the 11th of February, 1884, had no belief in a Supreme Being; 2nd, that he did not take and subscribe the oath in the sense of the Act, or according to the course and practice of Parliament.

The Court thereupon directed the jury to find a verdict for the Crown.

A motion by Mr. Bradlaugh for a new trial, and in arrest of Judgment, was refused by a Divisional Court (Dec. 8th), formed of the same judges.

Mr. Bradlaugh appealed from this refusal, but the appeal was dismissed by the Court of Appeal, composed of the *Master of the Rolls, Cotton,* and *Lindley,* LL.JJ.

Appendix.

Held:—(1) That the oath had not been taken and subscribed publicly and solemnly in accordance with the Act and the Standing Orders. (2) That a person who has not a belief in a Supreme Being cannot take an oath.

Note.—This case is added not as a great constitutional case, but because the reader may expect to find it here. As will be seen, it turns chiefly on the construction to be placed on the Act of Parliament, which must be read in connection with the practice of Parliament and the Standing Orders.

The sections of the Act of 1866 are as follows:—

'3. The Oath hereby appointed shall in every Parliament be solemnly and publicly made and subscribed by every Member of the .... House of Commons at the Table in the Middle of the said House, and whilst a full House of Commons is there duly sitting, with their Speaker in his Chair, at such hours and according to such Regulations as each House may by its Standing Orders direct.

'4. Every Person of the Persuasion of the People called Quakers and every other Person for the time being by law permitted to make a solemn Affirmation or Declaration instead of taking and subscribing the Oath hereby appointed, may make and subscribe a solemn Affirmation,' &c., &c.

The Standing Order of 30 April, 1866, directs that 'Members may take the oath at any time before the orders of the day or notices of motion are entered upon, or after they are disposed of, but no debate or business is to be interrupted for that purpose.'

There was an incidental question whether the action to recover the penalty was a criminal proceeding (in which case there would have been no right of appeal), but the Court of Appeal held that it was not.

The question upon the 4th section of this Act whether Mr. Bradlaugh was entitled, as he had originally claimed, to make an affirmation was decided against him in 1881 in the case of *Clarke v. Bradlaugh* in the Court of Appeal (L. R., 7 Q. B. D. 38). For an account of the several stages of Mr. Bradlaugh's attempt to take his seat, see May, P. P., 9th ed., 210, 212–215.

GENERAL INDEX.

ACT OF STATE,
Question for the Court, 80
But not for a jury, 81
Ratification may make an, 91

ADVOCATES,
No action against, for anything said or done in Court, 105

ALIENS,
Post-nati held not to be, 48
Rights of, 49

ALLEGIANCE,
Definition and doctrines of, 48, 49

BANKERS,
Loan to Charles II., 51

BILL OF EXCEPTIONS,
Judge finable for refusing, 102

BILL OF RIGHTS,
Abolished the dispensing power, 27

BISHOPS, SEVEN,
Points of law involved in their case, 18, 19

CHANCELLOR, LORD. *See* JUDGES.

COLONIAL GOVERNOR,
May be sued in this country, 76
Or in his own courts, 78, 80
Limit of his authority, 77

COLONIAL GOVERNOR—*continued.*
  May consent to an Act of Indemnity to himself, 79
  Court will decide what is an Act of State, 80
  See NOTE VI., 84

COLONIAL LEGISLATURE,
  And the *lex et consuetudo parliamenti*, 38

COMMANDER,
  Liability of, 87, 90, 91
  See NOTE VII., 92

CONSTITUTIONAL LAW,
  Its nature and object, 1, 2
  Its relation to Common Law, 2, 3

CONSTITUTIONAL POWERS,
  Their nature and exercise, 3

CONTEMPT: *See* HOUSES OF PARLIAMENT.

COURT MARTIAL,
  And the law courts, 86, 87, 88

CROWN,
  Its powers, 5, 7
  May use patent inventions without compensation, 12, 53
  May not change the laws, 13
  Its powers in colonies, 50
  These when once delegated cannot be resumed, 50
  Held entitled to alienate its revenues, 51
  No action against, for negligence of its servants, 52
  Nor generally for a trespass, 53
  Remedies against the, NOTE IV., 55
  Injurious grant, how remedied, 56
    See SOVEREIGN.

CUSTOM,
  " Child of the Common Law," 21

DECLARATION OF INDULGENCE
  Issued by James II., 16, 17

DISPENSATION,
  By licence or letters patent, 14, 15

DISPENSING POWER,
    How limited and restrained, 11, 14, 15, 17
    See NOTE I., 27

DOUBLE RETURN,
    At Common Law, and by Statute, 28

EXECUTIVE,
    Power of, how exercised, 3
    How far protected, 9

FORCED LOANS,
    Declared illegal, 57

GENERAL WARRANTS,
    Declared to be illegal, 67, 68
    As to papers illegal, 69
    See NOTE V., 70

GOVERNOR, COLONIAL : *See* COLONIAL.

GRANT FROM THE CROWN,
    How rescinded when injurious, 56
    Of letters patent for inventions, 12

HABEAS CORPUS,
    Act when passed, 57
    Judge finable for refusing writ of, in vacation, 102

HOUSE OF COMMONS,
    Held sole judge of the right of elections, 29, 31
    Commitment for contempt by, 38, 42, 43

HOUSES OF PARLIAMENT,
    Power to commit for contempt, 33, 38
    How far subject to law courts, 42, 43
    Members not accountable out of Parliament for words spoken in it, 34
    How far privilege extends to publication of speech, 36, 37
    And libellous publications, 40

HOUSES OF PARLIAMENT—*continued.*
Not subject to control of courts as to their own procedure, 44, 45
See NOTE II., 46

IMPARLANCE,
right of, claimed by the Seven Bishops, 19

IMPOSITIONS,
History and legality of, 20, 21

IMPRESSMENT,
Its history and legality, 65

IMPRISONMENT
Must be legal, 57

JUDGES,
Their influence in making law, 1
When liable to actions for judicial acts, 97—101
How removable, 103
See NOTE VIII., 102

JUDICIAL ACT, 100—103

JUDICIAL DECISIONS,
Their importance in making law, 1

JUDICIAL OFFICERS,
Immunity from action, 28, 32
See JUDGES.

JUDICIAL SYSTEM,
How guaranteed, 10

JURY,
May not be fined or imprisoned, 95, 96
Are not liable to action or indictment, 95, 97

JUSTICES OF THE PEACE,
Their liability for judicial acts, 102, 103

KING : *See* CROWN.

LAWS,
Crown cannot change the laws, 13
Or dispense with them, 14, 15, 17, 26

LEADING CASES,
　Meaning of, 4

LEGAL PROCEEDINGS,
　Report of, privileged, 109, 110

Lex et Consuetudo Parliamenti,
　And colonial legislatures, 36

LIBEL,
　Publication of speech made in parliament may be a, 36, 37
　Publication ordered by Parliament, may be a, 40

LIBERTY,
　Secured against the executive, 8, 57
　Exception to, in the case of impressment, 65

LORD CHANCELLOR: *See* JUDGES.

LORD LIEUTENANT OF IRELAND,
　Extent of his powers as viceroy, 81, 84

LORDS OF THE TREASURY,
　No mandamus lies to them to compel payment of monies as servants of the Crown, 54

MARTIAL LAW,
　Used in sense of military law, 86
　Whether it exists in England, 86

MAXIMS,
　The King can do no wrong, 7
　Nemo potest exuere patriam, 49

MILITARY COURTS,
　How far courts of law will interfere with, 86

MONOPOLIES,
　Void as against public policy, 11, 12

MONSTRANS DE DROIT,
　When employed, 55

NATURALISATION,
    History of law, 48, 49
NON OBSTANTE CLAUSE,
    Doctrine of, 14, 26

OFFICERS, MILITARY AND NAVAL,
    How far liable to their subordinates, 87, 88
    And to the public, 90, 91
    See NOTE VII., 92

PARLIAMENT : *See* HOUSES OF PARLIAMENT.
    Proceedings in, how far privileged, 108 ; cp. 36, 37
PARTIES TO AN ACTION,
    No action lies for anything said or done by, in Court, 104
PATENT, LETTERS, FOR INVENTIONS,
    How granted, 12
    How far good as against the Crown, 12, 53
PETITION, RIGHT TO,
    Its history, 18
PETITION OF GRIEVANCES,
    Account of, 22
PETITION OF RIGHT, 24
PETITIONS OF RIGHT,
    Proceedings on, 55
    See CROWN.

POSTMASTER-GENERAL,
    Not liable for negligence of his subordinates, 72
POST NATI,
    Held not aliens, 48
PREROGATIVE,
    Limited by law, 7, 13
PRIVILEGE OF PARLIAMENT,
    How far Parliament judge of, 40
    And the law courts, NOTE II., 46

Index. 121

PRIVILEGED COMMUNICATION,
  Between officers, 88, 89
PRIVY COUNCIL,
  Lords of, may not commit individually, 16, 69
PROCLAMATIONS,
  Power of Crown to make, how limited, 13
PROPERTY,
  Protected against the Crown, 21, 23, 55
PUBLIC MEETING,
  Report of, how far privileged, 111
PUBLIC OFFICERS,
  Not liable for default of their subordinates, 72
  Nor for contracts for the public service, 73
  Nor for acts done in their public character, 74, 75
PUBLICITY,
  Right of, 10, 108, 109, 110, 111

QUEEN : *See* CROWN.
QUEEN'S BENCH,
  Special jurisdiction over crimes committed by governors, 85

RETURNING OFFICER,
  Action against, for double return, 28
  For refusing a vote, 30
  Whether he is a judicial officer or not, 32

SCIRE FACIAS,
  To repeal grant from the Crown, 56
SECRETARY OF STATE,
  Power to commit, 67—69
  Power to issue general warrants, 67—69
  See NOTE V., 70
SEDITIOUS LIBEL,
  References for, 18
  General warrant for papers in case of, 69

SEDITIOUS WORDS,
    Spoken by member of House of Parliament in his place, not punishable out of Parliament, 34

SEIZURE OF PAPERS,
    General warrant for, illegal, 69, 70

SERJEANT-AT-ARMS,
    Action against, as officer of House of Commons, 43, 44, 45

SHERIFF,
    Action against returning officer, 28, 30
    How far a judicial officer, 25, 30, 32

SHIP-MONEY,
    History and legality of, 23

SHIP OF WAR,
    Treated as a floating island, 60

SLAVERY,
    How far a constitutional question, 58
    Law of England as to, 58—61
    Whether piracy by law of nations, 61

SOVEREIGN,
    May not try causes in person, 94
    See CROWN.

STAR CHAMBER,
    Practice of issuing general warrants, 70

SUBJECTS,
    Their duties to the Crown, 48
    Their remedies against the Crown, 55
    May resign or regain their nationality, 49

SUSPENDING POWER: *See* DISPENSING POWER.

TAXATION,
    Illegal without consent of Parliament, 5, 20, 23

TRIAL
    By jury how guaranteed, 95, 96

VICE-CHANCELLOR OF CAMBRIDGE,
    Has a special jurisdiction, 99

VICEROY,
    Extent of his powers, 9
    May not be sued in his own courts, 9, 81, 82
    At all events, not for an Act of State, 81—84
    See NOTE VI., 84

VILLEINAGE,
    Last cases of in English law, 63, 64
    Judges always leaned against, 64

WITNESSES,
    No action for anything said in giving evidence, 106, 107

THE END.

BRADBURY, AGNEW, & CO. LD., PRINTERS, WHITEFRIARS.

Telegraphic Address: "POLYGRAPHY, LONDON."

A CATALOGUE

OF

LAW WORKS

PUBLISHED AND SOLD BY

STEVENS & HAYNES,

𝕷𝖆𝖜 𝕻𝖚𝖇𝖑𝖎𝖘𝖍𝖊𝖗𝖘, 𝕭𝖔𝖔𝖐𝖘𝖊𝖑𝖑𝖊𝖗𝖘 & 𝕰𝖝𝖕𝖔𝖗𝖙𝖊𝖗𝖘,

13, BELL YARD, TEMPLE BAR, LONDON.

BOOKS BOUND IN THE BEST BINDINGS.

Works in all Classes of Literature supplied to Order.

FOREIGN BOOKS IMPORTED.

LIBRARIES VALUED FOR PROBATE, PARTNERSHIP, AND OTHER PURPOSES.

LIBRARIES OR SMALL COLLECTIONS OF BOOKS PURCHASED.

A large Stock of Reports of the various Courts of England, Ireland, and Scotland, always on hand.

Catalogues and Estimates Furnished, and Orders Promptly Executed.

NOTE.—*To avoid confusing our firm with any of a similar name, we beg to notify that we have no connexion whatever with any other house of business, and we respectfully request that Correspondents will take special care to direct all communications to the above names and address.*

INDEX OF SUBJECTS.

ABSTRACT DRAWING—
  Scott 32
ADMINISTRATION ACTIONS—
  Walker and Elgood. 18
ADMINISTRATORS—
  Walker. 6
ADMIRALTY LAW—
  Kay 17
  Smith 23
AFFILIATION—
  Martin 7
ARBITRATION—
  Slater 7
BANKRUPTCY—
  Baldwin 15
  Hazlitt 29
  Indermaur (Question & Answer) 28
  Ringwood 15, 29
BAR EXAMINATION JOURNAL 39
BIBLIOGRAPHY 40
BILLS OF EXCHANGE—
  Willis 14
BILLS OF LADING—
  Campbell 9
  Kay 17
BILLS OF SALE—
  Baldwin 15
  Indermaur 28
  Ringwood 15
BUILDING CONTRACTS—
  Hudson 12
CAPITAL PUNISHMENT—
  Copinger 42
CARRIERS—
  See RAILWAY LAW.
  ,, SHIPMASTERS.
CHANCERY DIVISION, Practice of—
  Brown's Edition of Snell . . 22
  Indermaur 25
  Williams 7
  And see EQUITY.
CHARITABLE TRUSTS—
  Cooke 10
  Whiteford 33
CHURCH AND CLERGY—
  Brice 9
CIVIL LAW—See ROMAN LAW.
CLUB LAW—
  Wertheimer 32
CODES—Argles 32
COLLISIONS AT SEA—Kay . 17
COLONIAL LAW—
  Cape Colony 38
  Forsyth 14
  Tarring 41
COMMERCIAL AGENCY—
  Campbell 9

COMMERCIAL LAW—
  Hurst and Cecil 11
COMMON LAW—
  Indermaur 24
COMPANIES LAW—
  Brice 16
  Buckley 17
  Reilly's Reports 29
  Smith 39
  Watts 47
COMPENSATION—
  Browne 19
  Lloyd 13
COMPULSORY PURCHASE—
  Browne 19
CONSTABLES—
  See POLICE GUIDE.
CONSTITUTIONAL LAW AND HISTORY—
  Forsyth 14
  Taswell-Langmead 21
  Thomas 28
CONSULAR JURISDICTION—
  Tarring 42
CONVEYANCING—
  Copinger, Title Deeds 45
  Copinger, Precedents in . . . 40
  Deane, Principles of 23
COPYRIGHT—
  Copinger 45
CORPORATIONS—
  Brice 16
  Browne 19
COSTS, Crown Office—
  Short 41
COVENANTS FOR TITLE—
  Copinger 45
CREW OF A SHIP—
  Kay 17
CRIMINAL LAW—
  Copinger 42
  Harris 27
CROWN LAW—
  Forsyth 14
  Hall 30
  Kelyng 35
  Taswell-Langmead 21
  Thomas 28
CROWN OFFICE RULES—
  Short 10
CROWN PRACTICE—
  Corner 10
  Short and Mellor 10
CUSTOM AND USAGE—
  Browne 19
  Mayne 38
DAMAGES—
  Mayne 31
DICTIONARIES—
  Brown 26

INDEX OF SUBJECTS—continued.

	PAGE		PAGE
DIGESTS—		**HINDU LAW—**	
Law Magazine Quarterly Digest	37	Coghlan	28
Menzies' Digest of Cape Reports	38	Cunningham	38 and 42
DISCOVERY—Peile	7	Mayne	38
DIVORCE—Harrison	23	**HISTORY—**	
DOMESTIC RELATIONS—		Taswell-Langmead	21
Eversley	9	**HUSBAND AND WIFE—**	
DOMICIL—See PRIVATE INTERNATIONAL LAW.		Eversley	9
		INDEX TO PRECEDENTS—	
DUTCH LAW	38	Copinger	40
ECCLESIASTICAL LAW—		**INFANTS—**	
Brice	9	Eversley	9
Smith	23	Simpson	43
EDUCATION ACTS—		**INJUNCTIONS—**	
See MAGISTERIAL LAW.		Joyce	44
ELECTION LAW and PETITIONS—		**INSTITUTE OF THE LAW—**	
Hardcastle	33	Brown's Law Dictionary	26
O'Malley and Hardcastle	33	**INSURANCE—**	
Seager	47	Porter	6
EQUITY—		**INTERNATIONAL LAW—**	
Blyth	22	Clarke	45
Choyce Cases	35	Cobbett	43
Pemberton	32	Foote	36
Snell	22	Law Magazine	37
Story	43	**INTERROGATORIES—**	
Williams	7	Peile	7
EVIDENCE—		**INTOXICATING LIQUORS—**	
Phipson	20	See MAGISTERIAL LAW.	
EXAMINATION OF STUDENTS—		**JOINT STOCK COMPANIES—**	
Bar Examination Journal	39	See COMPANIES.	
Indermaur	24 and 25	**JUDGMENTS AND ORDERS—**	
Intermediate L.L.B.	21	Pemberton	18
EXECUTORS—		**JUDICATURE ACTS—**	
Walker and Elgood	6	Cunningham and Mattinson	7
EXTRADITION—		Indermaur	25
Clarke	45	Kelke	6
See MAGISTERIAL LAW.		**JURISPRUDENCE—**	
FACTORIES—		Forsyth	14
See MAGISTERIAL LAW.		Salmond	13
FISHERIES—		**JUSTINIAN'S INSTITUTES—**	
See MAGISTERIAL LAW.		Campbell	47
FIXTURES—Brown	33	Harris	20
FOREIGN LAW—		**LANDLORD AND TENANT—**	
Argles	32	Foa	11
Dutch Law	38	**LANDS CLAUSES CONSOLIDATION ACT—**	
Foote	36		
Pavitt	32	Lloyd	13
FORESHORE—		**LATIN MAXIMS**	28
Moore	30	**LAW DICTIONARY—**	
FORGERY—See MAGISTERIAL LAW.		Brown	26
FRAUDULENT CONVEYANCES—		**LAW MAGAZINE and REVIEW**	37
May	29	**LEADING CASES—**	
GAIUS INSTITUTES—		Common Law	25
Harris	20	Constitutional Law	28
GAME LAWS—		Equity and Conveyancing	25
See MAGISTERIAL LAW.		Hindu Law	28
GUARDIAN AND WARD—		International Law	43
Eversley	9	**LEADING STATUTES—**	
HACKNEY CARRIAGES—		Thomas	28
See MAGISTERIAL LAW.			

INDEX OF SUBJECTS—continued.

LEASES—
  Copinger 45
LEGACY AND SUCCESSION—
  Hanson. 10
LEGITIMACY AND MARRIAGE—
  See PRIVATE INTERNATIONAL LAW.
LICENSES—See MAGISTERIAL LAW.
LIFE ASSURANCE—
  Buckley 17
  Reilly 29
LIMITATION OF ACTIONS—
  Banning 42
LUNACY—
  Renton 10
  Williams 7
MAGISTERIAL LAW—
  Greenwood and Martin . . . 46
MAINE'S (SIR H.), WORKS OF—
  Evans' Theories and Criticisms . 20
MAINTENANCE AND DESERTION.
  Martin 7
MARRIAGE and LEGITIMACY—
  Foote 36
MARRIED WOMEN'S PROPERTY ACTS—
  Brown's Edition of Griffith . . 40
MASTER AND SERVANT—
  Eversley 9
MERCANTILE LAW 32
  Campbell 9
  Duncan 33
  Hurst and Cecil 11
  Slater 7
  See SHIPMASTERS.
MERCHANDISE MARKS—
  Daniel 42
MINES—
  Harris 47
MONEY LENDERS—
  Bellot and Willis 11
MORTMAIN—
  See CHARITABLE TRUSTS.
NATIONALITY—See PRIVATE INTERNATIONAL LAW.
NEGLIGENCE—
  Beven 8
  Campbell 40
NEGOTIABLE INSTRUMENTS—
  Willis 14
NEWSPAPER LIBEL—
  Elliott 14
OBLIGATIONS—
  Brown's Savigny 20
PARENT AND CHILD—
  Eversley 9
PARLIAMENT—
  Taswell-Langmead 21
  Thomas 28

PARTITION—
  Walker 43
PASSENGERS—
  See MAGISTERIAL LAW.
  ,, RAILWAY LAW.
PASSENGERS AT SEA—
  Kay 17
PATENTS—
  Daniel 42
  Frost 12
PAWNBROKERS—
  See MAGISTERIAL LAW.
PETITIONS IN CHANCERY AND LUNACY—
  Williams 7
PILOTS—
  Kay 17
POLICE GUIDE—
  Greenwood and Martin . . . 46
POLLUTION OF RIVERS—
  Higgins 30
PRACTICE BOOKS—
  Bankruptcy 15
  Companies Law . . . . 29 and 39
  Compensation 13
  Compulsory Purchase . . . 19
  Conveyancing 45
  Damages 31
  Ecclesiastical Law 9
  Election Petitions 33
  Equity . . . . . 7, 22 and 32
  Injunctions 44
  Magisterial 46
  Pleading, Precedents of . . 7
  Railways 14
  Railway Commission . . . 19
  Rating 19
  Supreme Court of Judicature . 25
PRACTICE STATUTES, ORDERS AND RULES—
  Emden 11
PRECEDENTS OF PLEADING—
  Cunningham and Mattinson . . 7
  Mattinson and Macaskie . . 7
PRIMOGENITURE—
  Lloyd 13
PRINCIPLES—
  Brice (Corporations) 16
  Browne (Rating) 19
  Deane (Conveyancing) . . . 23
  Harris (Criminal Law) . . . 27
  Houston (Mercantile) . . . 32
  Indermaur (Common Law) . . 24
  Joyce (Injunctions) 44
  Ringwood (Bankruptcy) . . 15
  Snell (Equity) 22
PRIVATE INTERNATIONAL LAW—
  Foote 36

INDEX OF SUBJECTS—continued.

PROBATE—
  Hanson 10
  Harrison 23
PROMOTERS—
  Watts 47
PUBLIC WORSHIP—
  Brice 33
QUARTER SESSIONS—
  Smith (F. J.) 6
QUEEN'S BENCH DIVISION, Practice of—
  Indermaur 25
QUESTIONS FOR STUDENTS—
  Aldred 21
  Bar Examination Journal . . . 39
  Indermaur 25
  Waite 22
RAILWAYS—
  Browne 19
  Godefroi and Shortt 47
RATING—
  Browne 19
REAL PROPERTY—
  Deane 23
  Edwards 16
  Tarring 26
RECORDS—
  Inner Temple 11
REGISTRATION—
  Elliott (Newspaper) 14
  Seager (Parliamentary) 47
REPORTS—
  Bellewe 34
  Brooke 35
  Choyce Cases 35
  Cooke 35
  Cunningham 34
  Election Petitions 33
  Finlason 32
  Gibbs, Seymour Will Case . . 10
  Kelyng, John 35
  Kelynge, William 35
  Reilly 29
  Shower (Cases in Parliament) . 34
ROMAN DUTCH LAW—
  Van Leeuwen 38
ROMAN LAW—
  Brown's Analysis of Savigny . 20
  Campbell 47
  Harris 20
  Salkowski 14
  Whitfield 14
SALVAGE—
  Jones 47
  Kay 17
SAVINGS BANKS—
  Forbes 18
SCINTILLAE JURIS—
  Darling (C. J.) 18

SEA SHORE—
  Hall 30
  Moore 30
SHIPMASTERS AND SEAMEN—
  Kay 17
SOCIETIES—
  See CORPORATIONS.
STAGE CARRIAGES—
  See MAGISTERIAL LAW.
STAMP DUTIES—
  Copinger . . . . . 40 and 45
STATUTE OF LIMITATIONS—
  Banning 42
STATUTES—
  Craies 9
  Hardcastle 9
  Marcy 26
  Thomas 28
STOPPAGE IN TRANSITU—
  Campbell 9
  Houston 32
  Kay 17
STUDENTS' BOOKS . 20—28, 39, 47
SUCCESSION DUTIES—
  Hanson 10
SUCCESSION LAWS—
  Lloyd 13
SUPREME COURT OF JUDICATURE, Practice of—
  Cunningham and Mattinson . . 7
  Indermaur 25
TELEGRAPHS—
  See MAGISTERIAL LAW.
TITLE DEEDS—
  Copinger 45
TORTS—
  Ringwood 13
TRADE MARKS—
  Daniel 42
TREASON—
  Kelyng 35
  Taswell-Langmead 21
TRIALS—Bartlett, A. (Murder) . . 32
  Queen v. Gurney 32
ULTRA VIRES—
  Brice 16
USAGES AND CUSTOMS—
  Browne 19
  Mayne 38
VOLUNTARY CONVEYANCES—
  May 29
WATER COURSES—
  Higgins 30
WILLS, CONSTRUCTION OF—
  Gibbs, Report of Wallace v. Attorney-General 10
WORKING CLASSES, Housing of
  Lloyd 13

Third Edition, in 8vo, price 21s., cloth,

THE LAWS OF INSURANCE:
Fire, Life, Accident, and Guarantee.
EMBODYING
CASES IN THE ENGLISH, SCOTCH, IRISH, AMERICAN, AND CANADIAN COURTS.
By JAMES BIGGS PORTER,
OF THE INNER TEMPLE, BARRISTER-AT-LAW.
ASSISTED BY
W. FEILDEN CRAIES, M.A., AND THOMAS S. LITTLE,
OF THE INNER TEMPLE, BARRISTERS-AT-LAW.

"In reviewing the first edition of this book we expressed an opinion that it was a painstaking and useful work. Its utility has been shown by the speedy appearance of the present edition, and the labour of its authors is still apparent to anyone who will glance through its pages."—*Solicitors' Journal.*

"The success of the first edition proves its value. It is clearly and concisely compiled, and upwards of 1,500 cases are quoted."—*Law Times.*

"Mr. Porter's useful book on Insurance law has reached a second edition in less than three years, which is not common in a book of this class. The fact is, that in taking up insurance law in all its branches, except marine insurance, he hits upon a popular subject. . . . . Mr. Porter well fills the gap thus made for him, and he has called to his aid a useful coadjutor in the person of Mr. Craies."—*Law Journal.*

"When writing on the first edition in 1884, we ventured to predict for Mr. Porter's work a great success. We spoke in terms of unqualified commendation concerning the lucidity of the author's style, the thoroughness of his work and his happy gift of narrowing down broad and diffusive subjects into a small space. Practical experience of the contents of the volume during the past three years has, we may say, fully confirmed our favourable views."—*Insurance Record.*

In Royal 12mo, price 20s., cloth,

QUARTER SESSIONS PRACTICE,
A VADE MECUM OF GENERAL PRACTICE IN APPELLATE AND CIVIL CASES AT QUARTER SESSIONS.
By FREDERICK JAMES SMITH,
OF THE MIDDLE TEMPLE, BARRISTER-AT-LAW, AND RECORDER OF MARGATE.

Third Edition. In one volume, 8vo, price 21s., cloth,

A COMPENDIUM OF THE LAW RELATING TO EXECUTORS AND ADMINISTRATORS, With an Appendix of
Statutes, Annotated by means of References to the Text. By W. GREGORY WALKER, B.A., Barrister-at-Law, and EDGAR J. ELGOOD, B.C.L., M.A., Barrister-Law. Third Edition by E. J. ELGOOD, B.C.L., M.A.

"We highly approve of Mr. Walker's arrangement. . . . . The Notes are full, and as far as we have been able to ascertain, carefully and accurately compiled. . . . . . We can commend it as bearing on its face evidence of skilful and careful labour, and we anticipate that it will be found a very acceptable substitute for the ponderous tomes of the much esteemed and valued Williams."—*Law Times.*

"Mr. Walker is fortunate in his choice of a subject, and the power of treating it succinctly ; for the ponderous tomes of Williams, however satisfactory as an authority, are necessarily inconvenient for reference as well as expensive. . . . . . On the whole we are inclined to think the book a good and useful one."—*Law Journal.*

In royal 12mo, price 4s., cloth,

A DIGEST OF THE LAW OF
PRACTICE UNDER THE JUDICATURE ACTS AND RULES,
AND THE CASES DECIDED IN THE CHANCERY AND COMMON LAW DIVISIONS FROM NOVEMBER 1875 TO AUGUST 1880.
By W. H. HASTINGS KELKE, M.A., Barrister-at-Law.

Second Edition, in 8vo, price 9s., cloth,

THE LAW OF MAINTENANCE AND DESERTION,

AND THE ORDERS OF THE JUSTICES THEREON. Second Edition, including the LAW OF AFFILIATION and BASTARDY. With an Appendix of Statutes and Forms, including the Summary Jurisdiction (Married Womens') Act of, 1895. By TEMPLE CHEVALLIER MARTIN, Chief Clerk of the Lambeth Police Court, Editor of the "Magisterial and Police Guide," &c., and GEORGE TEMPLE MARTIN, M.A., of Lincoln's Inn, Barrister-at-Law.

Third Edition. Crown 8vo, in preparation,

THE LAW OF ARBITRATION AND AWARDS;

With Appendix containing Lord Denman's ARBITRATION BILL, AND STATUTES RELATING TO ARBITRATION, and a collection of Forms and Index. Second Edition. With a Supplement containing an Abstract of the Arbitration Act, 1889. By JOSHUA SLATER, of Gray's Inn, Barrister-at-Law.

₊ *The Supplement can be had separately, price 6d.*

In crown 8vo, price 6s., cloth,

THE PRINCIPLES OF MERCANTILE LAW. By

JOSHUA SLATER, of Gray's Inn, Barrister-at-Law.

In 8vo, price 12s., cloth,

THE LAW AND PRACTICE OF DISCOVERY in

the SUPREME COURT of JUSTICE. WITH AN APPENDIX OF FORMS, ORDERS, &c., AND AN ADDENDA GIVING THE ALTERATIONS UNDER THE NEW RULES OF PRACTICE. By CLARENCE J. PEILE, of the Inner Temple, Barrister-at-Law.

In one volume, 8vo, price 18s., cloth,

THE LAW AND PRACTICE RELATING TO

PETITIONS IN CHANCERY AND LUNACY,

INCLUDING THE SETTLED ESTATES ACT, LANDS CLAUSES ACT, TRUSTEE ACT, WINDING-UP PETITIONS, PETITIONS RELATING TO SOLICITORS, INFANTS, ETC., ETC. WITH AN APPENDIX OF FORMS AND PRECEDENTS. By SYDNEY E. WILLIAMS, Barrister-at-Law.

Second Edition, in 8vo, price 28s., cloth,

A SELECTION OF PRECEDENTS OF PLEADING

UNDER THE JUDICATURE ACTS IN THE COMMON LAW DIVISIONS.
With Notes explanatory of the different Causes of Action and Grounds of Defence ; and an Introductory Treatise on the Present Rules and Principles of Pleading as illustrated by the various Decisions down to the Present Time.

By J. CUNNINGHAM and M. W. MATTINSON.

SECOND EDITION.

BY MILES WALKER MATTINSON, of Gray's Inn, Barrister-at-Law, and STUART CUNNINGHAM MACASKIE, of Gray's Inn, Barrister-at-Law.

REVIEWS.

"The notes are very pertinent and satisfactory: the introductory chapters on the present system of pleading are excellent, and the precedents will be found very useful."—*Irish Law Times.*
"A work which, in the compass of a single portable volume, contains a brief Treatise on the Principles and Rules of Pleading, and a carefully annotated body of Forms which have to a great extent gone through the entirely separate sifting processes of Chambers Court, and Judges' Chambers, cannot fail to be a most useful companion in the Practitioner's daily routine."—*Law Magazine and Review.*

Second Edition, in two volumes, royal 8vo, price 70s., cloth.

NEGLIGENCE IN LAW

BEING THE SECOND EDITION OF "PRINCIPLES OF THE LAW OF NEGLIGENCE,"
RE-ARRANGED AND RE-WRITTEN.

By THOMAS BEVEN,

OF THE INNER TEMPLE, BARRISTER-AT-LAW; AUTHOR OF 'THE LAW OF MPLOYERS' LIABILITY FOR THE NEGLIGENCE OF SERVANTS CAUSING INJURY TO FELLOW SERVANTS."

REVIEWS.

"These volumes, says Mr. Beven in the preface, may be regarded as a recond edition of his 'Principles of the Law of Negligence,' in so far as the subjects treated of in both books are the same; and the materials collected in the one have been used without reserve in the other. As to anything beyond this, he continues, the present is a new work. The arrangement is altogether different from that previously adopted. 'Nearly a half of the contents of these volumes is absolutely new, and of the remainder there is very little which has not been materially modified, if not in substance, yet in expression.

"Upon its first appearance, the 'Principles of the Law of Negligence' was at once recognized as a work of the highest importance, and the ability and industry which Mr. Beven had brought to bear upon his task laid the profession under no ordinary obligation. The service which he then rendered has been greatly increased by the production of this second edition, and the book deserves a place in the first rank among authoritative expositions of the law.

"The chief characteristic of Mr. Beven s method is thoroughness. He is not himself in a hurry, and it is certainly useless for his readers to be so. The law is to be found in his pages, and, when found, it is clearly enunciated; but it is always deduced from a full and discriminating examination of multitudinous cases—English and American—and readers must be content to survey, leisurely and cautiously, with Mr. Beven, the whole field of judicial exposition, and to follow his own careful and elaborate criticism, if they would gain the full benefit of the results at which he arrives. The book is not meant to be taken up for a hasty reference, and often the lawyer may find it more convenient to resort to a treatise more concise. On the other hand, it will be an invaluable companion in the consideration of any matter which requires research, and the style and arrangement are such that, whether the book is used for purposes of business or of general study, it cannot fail to prove deeply interesting. . . .

"The above account is but a sketch of Mr. Beven's great work. It is impossible within the present limits to give an adequate idea of the variety of topics which are included, of the learning and patience with which they are discussed. Negligence may only be an aspect of the law; but the treatment here accorded to it throws into prominence a host of questions of the utmost importance, both practically and theoretically. By his contribution to the due understanding of these Mr. Beven has placed the profession under a lasting obligation, an obligation which no reader of his work will fail to realize."—*Solicitors' Journal.*

"The book upon which this is founded, and which is in a measure a former edition of the present volumes, has made Mr. Beven an authority on the subject of the law of negligence. He has, in writing these volumes, made full use of his former labours, but he claims that in reality the present work is a new one, and his claim is justified. . . . Just occasionally a well-written and ably-conceived law book is published, and such a one is this of Mr. Beven's. We think that to compare it with other books on the subject would be impossible; it stands easily the best book on the subject. In clear exposition of law, for good classification of subject-matter, for accuracy of detail, and for every arrangement to facilitate reference it cannot be beaten. We may congratulate Mr. Beven upon the accomplishment of his laborious task; he has given to the profession a valuable work, and one which will enhance his reputation as a writer on the Law of Negligence."—*Law Journal,* August 3, 1895.

"He has treated the well-known subject of Negligence in a scientific way, and has not been content with merely collecting, in more or less relevant positions, a number of cases which anyone could find for himself in any Digest of Law Reports, but has endeavoured to reduce from the chaos of decided cases a systematic study of the subject, with clear enunciations of the principles he finds governing the various decisions. In the arrangement of the book the author has been very happy in his method, a by no means easy task in the treatment of a subject in which each branch of it in reality overlaps another. . . . A good index and clear type increase the value of a book which will without doubt receive the hearty commendation of the profession as a successful completion of the author's ambitious task."—*Law Times.*

"In respect of the style of treatment of the subject, the book must be highly commended. It will be of service to every lawyer who wishes rather to get an intelligent understanding of the Law of Negligence, than merely to find correct and reliable legal propositions for practical use, and that whether he be a student or a practitioner. To the student the work is valuable for the searching and well-sustained discussion of the cases; and to the practitioner there are presented all the cases that bear on most points for which he may be in search of authority. One of the chief merits of the work is, that all the available authority on each point is collected and so arranged that it can be easily found."—*Juridical Review.*

"Contains evidence of much serious work, and ought to receive a fair trial at the hands of the profession.'—*Law Quarterly Review.*

Second Edition, in royal 8vo, price 38s., cloth,

THE LAW OF THE DOMESTIC RELATIONS,
INCLUDING
HUSBAND AND WIFE: PARENT AND CHILD: GUARDIAN AND
WARD: INFANTS: AND MASTER AND SERVANT.

By WILLIAM PINDER EVERSLEY, B.C.L., M.A.,
OF THE INNER TEMPLE, BARRISTER-AT-LAW.

"We are glad to see a second edition of Mr. Eversley's useful work. There is a convenience in having the various subjects of which it treats collected in one volume, while at the same time each is handled with such fulness as to give the reader all the information he could expect in a separate volume. Mr. Eversley states the law with the most painstaking thoroughness, and has made an exhaustive survey of all the relevant statutes and cases. . . Great care has been taken to make the present edition complete and accurate, and a very full index adds to its utility."—*Solicitors' Journal.*

"Important statutes and cases have come into operation since the first edition, and this has induced Mr. Eversley to give the contracts of married women separate treatment. Careful revision to date now makes this treatise comprehensive and thoroughly reliable."—*Law Times.*

"This is an important and almost a leading treatise on domestic law. The former edition was received with merited favour. Its value has become well known, and now, after an interval of eleven years, the learned author has brought out a second edition."—*Law Journal.*

"It is only necessary to refer to Mr. Eversley's learned and scholarlike work on 'The Domestic Relations,' a book which, though technically belonging to the forbidding ranks of 'Law Books,' is yet full of human interest, and written, moreover, in the English language."—*Edinburgh Review.*

Second Edition, in one volume, royal 8vo, price 32s., cloth,

THE LAW RELATING TO THE
SALE OF GOODS AND COMMERCIAL AGENCY.
SECOND EDITION.

By ROBERT CAMPBELL, M.A.,
OF LINCOLN'S INN, BARRISTER-AT-LAW; ADVOCATE OF THE SCOTCH BAR.
AUTHOR OF THE "LAW OF NEGLIGENCE," ETC.

"An accurate, careful, and exhaustive handbook on the subject with which it deals. The excellent index deserves a special word of commendation."—*Law Quarterly Review.*

"We can, therefore, repeat what we said when reviewing the first edition—that the book is a contribution of value to the subject treated of, and that the writer deals with his subject carefully and fully."—*Law Journal.*

Second Edition, in one volume, 8vo, price 28s., cloth,

A TREATISE ON
THE CONSTRUCTION AND EFFECT OF STATUTE LAW.
WITH APPENDICES CONTAINING WORDS AND EXPRESSIONS USED IN STATUTES
WHICH HAVE BEEN JUDICIALLY OR STATUTABLY CONSTRUED, AND
THE POPULAR AND SHORT TITLES OF CERTAIN STATUTES.

By HENRY HARDCASTLE, BARRISTER-AT-LAW.
SECOND EDITION, REVISED AND ENLARGED, BY W. F. CRAIES,
BARRISTER-AT-LAW.

"The result of Mr. Craies' industry is a sound and good piece of work, the new light thrown on the subject since 1879 having been blended with the old in a thoroughly workmanlike manner. Though less a student's manual than a practitioner's text book, it is the sort of volume an intelligent perusal of which would educate a student better than the reading of much substantial law."—*Saturday Review.*

Fourth Edition, in 8vo, price 30s., cloth,

HANSON'S DEATH DUTIES; being the Fourth Edition of
the Acts relating to Estate Duty Finance, Probate, Legacy, and Succession Duties. Comprising the 36 Geo. III. c. 52; 45 Geo. III. c. 28; 55 Geo. III. c. 184; and 16 & 17 Vict. c. 51; the Customs and Inland Revenue Acts, 43 Vict. c. 14; and 44 Vict. c. 12; also the New Estate Duty Finance Acts, 57 & 58 Vict. c. 30, and 59 & 60 Vict. c. 28; with an Introduction, Copious Notes, and References to all the Decided Cases in England, Scotland, and Ireland. An Appendix and a full Index. By ALFRED HANSON, of the Middle Temple, Esq., Barrister-at-Law, Comptroller of Legacy and Succession Duties. Fourth Edition by LEWIS T. DIBDIN, M.A., D.C.L., and F. H. L. ERRINGTON, M.A., Barristers-at-Law.

"It is remarkable how surely a really good legal treatise finds favour with the Profession. The late Mr. Hanson's edition of the Acts relating to "Estate, Probate, Legacy and Succession Duties," is one of these. . . . . The passing of the Finance Acts of 1894 and 1896 have caused the introduction of new matter. We recognise a decided improvement in the work, which we think will enhance its reputation with the Profession, and all interested in a somewhat difficult subject."—*Law Times.*

"Of all the various treatises on the subject to which the recent Acts have given birth, the one under review strikes us as the fullest and best, and we heartily recommend it to all seeking instruction on these difficult statutes."—*Irish Law Times.*

In one Volume, royal 8vo, price 50s. net,

THE LAW AND PRACTICE IN LUNACY; with
the Lunacy Acts, 1890-91 (Consolidated and Annotated); the Rules of Lunacy Commissioners; the Idiots Act, 1886; the Vacating of Seats Act, 1886; the Rules in Lunacy; the Lancashire County (Asylums and other powers) Act, 1891; the Inebriates Act, 1879 and 1888 (Consolidated and Annotated); the Criminal Lunacy Acts, 1800-1884; and a Collection of Forms, Precedents, &c. By A. WOOD RENTON, Barrister-at-Law.

In 8vo, price 30s., cloth,

THE PRACTICE ON THE CROWN SIDE
Of the Queen's Bench Division of Her Majesty's High Court of Justice
(Founded on CORNER'S CROWN OFFICE PRACTICE), including
APPEALS FROM INFERIOR COURTS; WITH APPENDICES OF RULES AND FORMS.

BY F. H. SHORT, Chief Clerk of the Crown Office, and
FRANCIS HAMILTON MELLOR, M.A., Barrister-at-Law.

In 8vo, price 12s., cloth,

THE CROWN OFFICE RULES AND FORMS, 1886.
The Supreme Court of Judicature Acts and Rules of the Supreme Court, 1883, relating to the Practice on the Crown side of the Queen's Bench Division; including Appeals from Inferior Courts, Tables of Court Fees, Scales of Costs; together with Notes, Cases, and a Full Index. By F. H. SHORT, Chief Clerk of the Crown Office.

In royal 8vo, 1877, price 10s., cloth,

THE CASE OF LORD HENRY SEYMOUR'S WILL
(WALLACE *v.* THE ATTORNEY-GENERAL).
Reported by FREDERICK WAYMOUTH GIBBS, C.B., Barrister-at-Law,
LATE FELLOW OF TRINITY COLLEGE, CAMBRIDGE.

In 8vo, 1867, price 16s., cloth,

CHARITABLE TRUSTS ACTS, 1853, 1855, 1860;
THE CHARITY COMMISSIONERS' JURISDICTION ACT, 1862;
THE ROMAN CATHOLIC CHARITIES ACTS:
Together with a Collection of Statutes relating to or affecting Charities, including the Mortmain Acts, Notes of Cases from 1853 to the present time, Forms of Declarations of Trust, Conditions of Sale, and Conveyance of Charity Land, and a very copious Index. Second Edition.
By HUGH COOKE and R. G. HARWOOD, of the Charity Commission.

Just Published, Demy 8vo, 152 pp. Price 7s. 6d.

THE LAW RELATING TO
UNCONSCIONABLE BARGAINS
WITH
MONEY-LENDERS.

INCLUDING the History of Usury to the Repeal of the Usury Laws, with Appendices, containing a Digest of Cases, Annotated; relating to Unconscionable Bargains, Statutes, and Forms for the use of Practitioners. By HUGH H. L. BELLOT, M.A., B.C.L., and R. JAMES WILLIS, Barristers-at-Law.

INNER TEMPLE RECORDS. A Calendar of the. Edited by F. A. INDERWICK, Q.C. Vol. I., 21 Hen. VII. (1505)—45 Eliz. (1603). Imperial 8vo. Roxburghe binding. 1896. 20s. net.

In one Volume, 8vo, price 20s., cloth,

THE
PRINCIPLES OF COMMERCIAL LAW;
WITH AN APPENDIX OF STATUTES, ANNOTATED BY MEANS OF REFERENCES TO THE TEXT.

By JOSEPH HURST AND LORD ROBERT CECIL,
OF THE INNER TEMPLE, BARRISTERS-AT-LAW.

"Their compendium, we believe, will be found a really useful volume, one for the lawyer and the business man to keep at his elbow, and which, if not giving them all that they require, will place in their hands the key to the richer and more elaborate treasures of the Law which lie in larger and more exhaustive works."—*Law Times.*

"The object of the authors of this work, they tell us in their preface, is to state, within a moderate compass, the principles of commercial law. Very considerable pains have obviously been expended on the task, and the book is in many respects a very serviceable one."—*Law Journal.*

Second Edition, in royal 8vo, price 25s., cloth,

THE
RELATIONSHIP OF LANDLORD AND TENANT.
By EDGAR FOA,
OF THE INNER TEMPLE, BARRISTER-AT-LAW.

"Will be found of much value to practitioners, and when a second edition has given the author the opportunity of reconsidering and carefully revising his statements in detail, we think it will take its place as a very good treatise on the modern law of landlord and tenant."—*Solicitors' Journal.*

"Mr. Foa is a bold man to undertake the exposition of a branch of law so full of difficulties and encumbered by so many decisions as the Law of Landlord and Tenant. But his boldness is justified by the excellent arrangement and by the lucid statements which characterise his book."—*Law Quarterly Review.*

"Mr. Foa's is a compact work, treating (1) of the creation of the relationship; (2) the incidents of creation (distress) and determination of the relationship; (3) modes and incidents of determination. We commend it to the attention of the Profession and predict for Foa on Landlord and Tenant a very useful and very permanent future."—*Law Times.*

"We have nothing but praise for the work, and we shall be astonished if it does not rank in course of time as one of the best—if not the best—work for every-day practice on the subject of Landlord and Tenant."—*Law Notes.*

"Without making any invidious comparison with existing works on the subject, we may frankly say that Mr. Foa's work indisputably possesses merit. . . . Our verdict on the book must be a decidedly favourable one."—*Law Students' Journal.*

"'The Relationship of Landlord and Tenant,' written by Mr. Edgar Foa, Barrister-at-Law, affords a striking instance of accuracy and lucidity of statement. The volume should be found useful not only by lawyers but by landlords and tenants themselves, the law in each particular being stated with a simplicity and clearness which bring it within the grasp of the lay mind."—*Law Gazette.*

Second Edition. In royal 8vo, nearly ready,

A TREATISE ON THE

LAW AND PRACTICE
RELATING TO
LETTERS PATENT FOR INVENTIONS.
WITH AN
APPENDIX OF STATUTES, INTERNATIONAL CONVENTION,
RULES, FORMS AND PRECEDENTS, ORDERS, &c.

By ROBERT FROST, B.Sc. (LOND.),
FELLOW OF THE CHEMICAL SOCIETY; OF LINCOLN'S INN, ESQUIRE, BARRISTER-AT-LAW.

"In our view a good piece of work may create a demand, and without disparaging existing literature upon the subject of patents, we think the care and skill with which the volume by Mr. Frost has been compiled entitles it to recognition at the hands of the profession. . . . Judging Mr. Frost on this ground, we find him completely satisfactory. A careful examination of the entire volume satisfies us that great care and much labour have been devoted to the production of this treatise, and we think that patent agents, solicitors, the bar and the bench, may confidently turn for guidance and instruction to the pages of Mr. Frost."—*Law Times.*

"Few practice books contain so much in so reasonable a space, and we repeat that it will be found generally useful by practitioners in this important branch of the law. . . . A capital index concludes the book."—*Law Journal.*

"The book is, as it professes to be, a treatise on patent law and practice, the several topics being conveniently arranged and discussed in the thirteen chapters which the body of the work, to which are appended statutes, rules, and forms. The statements of the law, so far as we have been able to test them, appear to be clear and accurate, and the author's style is pleasant and good. . . . The book is a good one, and will make its way. The index is better than usual. Both paper and type are also excellent."—*Solicitors' Journal.*

Second Edition. In two volumes, royal 8vo, price 50s., cloth,

A PRACTICAL TREATISE ON THE

LAW OF BUILDING AND ENGINEERING CONTRACTS,
AND OF THE DUTIES AND LIABILITIES OF ENGINEERS, ARCHITECTS,
SURVEYORS AND VALUERS,
WITH AN APPENDIX OF PRECEDENTS,
ANNOTATED BY MEANS OF REFERENCE TO THE TEXT AND TO CONTRACTS
IN USE.

AND AN APPENDIX OF UNREPORTED CASES
ON BUILDING AND ENGINEERING CONTRACTS.

By ALFRED A. HUDSON,
OF THE INNER TEMPLE, BARRISTER-AT-LAW.

"This is a book of great elaboration and completeness. It appears from the preface that the author has the twofold qualification of technical knowledge of building, gained as an architect, and devotion to the legal aspects of building, engineering, and shipbuilding contracts since he became a member of the bar. . . . The list of cases cited covers fifty large pages, and they include, not merely English, but American and Colonial decisions. . . . The book as a whole represents a large amount of well-directed labour, and it ought to become the standard work on its subject."—*Solicitors' Journal.*

"A very full index completes the book. Mr. Hudson has struck out a new line for himself, and produced a work of considerable merit, and one which will probably be found indispensable by practitioners, inasmuch as it contains a great deal that is not to be found elsewhere. The Table of Cases refers to all the reports."—*Law Journal.*

"Mr. Hudson, having abandoned his profession of an architect to become a barrister, hit upon the idea of writing this work, and he has done it with a thoroughness which every housewoner would like to see bestowed upon modern houses. . . . The Index and Table of Cases reveal a vast amount of industry expended upon detail, and we shall be much surprised if Mr. Hudson does not reap the reward of his labours by obtaining a large and appreciative public."—*Law Times.*

Third Edition. In 8vo, price 10s. 6d., cloth,

OUTLINES OF THE LAW OF TORTS.

By RICHARD RINGWOOD, M.A.,
OF THE MIDDLE TEMPLE, BARRISTER-AT-LAW; AUTHOR OF "PRINCIPLES OF BANKRUPTCY," &c.,
AND LECTURER ON COMMON LAW TO THE INCORPORATED LAW SOCIETY.

"This is a work by the well-known author of a student's book on Bankruptcy. Its groundwork is a series of lectures delivered in 1887 by Mr. Ringwood, as lecturer appointed by the Incorporated Law Society. It is clear, concise, well and intelligently written and one rises from its perusal with feelings of pleasure. . . . After perusing the entire work, we can conscientiously recommend it to students."—*Law Students' Journal.*

"The work is one we well recommend to law students, and the able way in which it is written reflects much credit upon the author."—*Law Times.*

"Mr. Ringwood's book is a plain and straightforward introduction to this branch of the law."—*Law Journal.*

. *Prescribed as a text-book by the Incorporated Law Society of Ireland.*

Sixth Edition, in 8vo, price 21s., cloth,

THE LAW OF COMPENSATION FOR LANDS, HOUSES, &c.

UNDER THE LANDS CLAUSES CONSOLIDATION ACTS, THE RAILWAYS CLAUSES CONSOLIDATION ACTS, THE PUBLIC HEALTH ACT, 1875; THE HOUSING OF THE WORKING CLASSES ACT, 1890; THE METROPOLIS LOCAL MANAGEMENT ACT
AND OTHER ACTS,

WITH A FULL COLLECTION OF FORMS AND PRECEDENTS.

By EYRE LLOYD,
OF THE INNER TEMPLE, BARRISTER-AT-LAW.

SIXTH EDITION.

By W. J. BROOKS,
OF THE INNER TEMPLE, BARRISTER-AT-LAW.

"In providing the legal profession with a book which contains the decisions of the Courts of Law and Equity upon the various statutes relating to the Law of Compensation, Mr. Eyre Lloyd has long since left all competitors in the distance, and his book may now be considered the standard work upon the subject. The plan of Mr. Lloyd's book is generally known, and its lucidity is appreciated; the present quite fulfils all the promises of the preceding editions, and contains in addition to other matter a complete set of forms under the Artizans and Labourers Act, 1875, and specimens of Bills of Costs, which will be found a novel feature, extremely useful to legal practitioners."—JUSTICE OF THE PEACE.

In 8vo, price 7s., cloth,

THE SUCCESSION LAWS OF CHRISTIAN COUNTRIES,

WITH SPECIAL REFERENCE TO THE LAW OF PRIMOGENITURE AS IT EXISTS IN ENGLAND.

By EYRE LLOYD, B.A., Barrister-at-Law.

In crown 8vo, price 6s., cloth,

ESSAYS IN JURISPRUDENCE AND LEGAL HISTORY.

By JOHN W. SALMOND, M.A., LL.B. (LOND.),
A BARRISTER OF THE SUPREME COURT OF NEW ZEALAND.

In crown 8vo, price 6s., cloth.

THE FIRST PRINCIPLES OF JURISPRUDENCE.

By JOHN W. SALMOND, M.A., LL.B.,
BARRISTER-AT-LAW; AUTHOR OF "ESSAYS IN JURISPRUDENCE AND LEGAL HISTORY."

14   STEVENS & HAYNES, BELL YARD, TEMPLE BAR.

In 8vo, price 7s. 6d., cloth,

THE LAW OF

NEGOTIABLE SECURITIES.

CONTAINED IN A COURSE OF SIX LECTURES.

DELIVERED BY WILLIAM WILLIS, ESQ., Q.C.,

AT THE REQUEST OF

THE COUNCIL OF LEGAL EDUCATION.

In one large vol., 8vo, price 32s., cloth,

INSTITUTES AND HISTORY OF ROMAN PRIVATE LAW,
WITH CATENA OF TEXTS.

BY DR. CARL SALKOWSKI, Professor of Laws, Königsberg.

Translated and Edited by E. E. WHITFIELD, M.A. (Oxon.).

In 8vo, price 4s. 6d., cloth,

THE

NEWSPAPER LIBEL AND REGISTRATION ACT, 1881.

WITH A STATEMENT OF THE LAW OF LIBEL AS AFFECTING PROPRIETORS, PUBLISHERS, AND EDITORS OF NEWSPAPERS.

By G. ELLIOTT, Barrister-at-Law, of the Inner Temple.

In one volume, royal 8vo,

CASES AND OPINIONS ON CONSTITUTIONAL LAW,
AND VARIOUS POINTS OF ENGLISH JURISPRUDENCE.

COLLECTED AND DIGESTED FROM OFFICIAL DOCUMENTS AND OTHER SOURCES.

WITH NOTES.

By WILLIAM FORSYTH, M.A., M.P., Q.C.,
STANDING COUNSEL TO THE SECRETARY OF STATE IN COUNCIL OF INDIA,
Author of "Hortensius," "History of Trial by Jury," "Life of Cicero," etc.
late Fellow of Trinity College, Cambridge.

Sixth Edition, in 8vo, price 10s. 6d., cloth,

THE PRINCIPLES OF BANKRUPTCY.
WITH AN APPENDIX,
CONTAINING
THE CONSOLIDATED RULES OF 1886, 1890 & 1891, SCALE OF COSTS, AND THE BILLS OF SALE ACTS, 1878, 1882, 1890 & 1891, AND THE RULES THEREUNDER; THE DEEDS OF ARRANGEMENT ACT, 1887, AND THE RULES THEREUNDER.

By RICHARD RINGWOOD, M.A.,
OF THE MIDDLE TEMPLE, BARRISTER-AT-LAW; LATE SCHOLAR OF TRINITY COLLEGE, DUBLIN.

"We welcome a new edition of this excellent student's book. We have written favourably of it in reviewing previous editions, and every good word we have written we would now reiterate and perhaps even more so. . . . In conclusion, we congratulate Mr. Ringwood on this edition, and have no hesitation in saying that it is a capital student's book."—*Law Students' Journal.*

"This edition is a considerable improvement on the first, and although chiefly written for the use of Students, the work will be found useful to the practitioner."—*Law Times.*

Seventh Edition, in 8vo, price 21s., cloth,

A TREATISE UPON

THE LAW OF BANKRUPTCY
AND
BILLS OF SALE.
WITH AN APPENDIX
CONTAINING

THE BANKRUPTCY ACTS, 1883—1890; GENERAL RULES, FORMS, SCALE OF COSTS AND FEES; RULES UNDER S. 122 OF 1888; DEEDS OF ARRANGEMENT ACTS. 1887—1890; RULES AND FORMS; BOARD OF TRADE AND COURT ORDERS; DEBTORS ACTS, 1869, 1878; RULES AND FORMS; BILLS OF SALE ACTS, 1878—1891, ETC., ETC.

By EDWARD T. BALDWIN, M.A.,
OF THE INNER TEMPLE, BARRISTER-AT-LAW.

"The seven editions simply record the constant progress of case growth and statute law. It is a remarkably useful compendium."—*Law Times,* July 20, 1895.
"As a well-arranged and complete collection of case law this book should be found of great use."—*Law Journal,* July 20, 1895.
"Carefully brought down to date."—*Solicitors' Journal,* November 9, 1895.
"We have always considered the work an admirable one, and the present edition is quite up to the previous high standard of excellence. We know of no better book on bankruptcy for the practitioner's library."—*Law Students' Journal,* August, 1895.
"Practitioners may, we feel sure, safely rely on its accuracy. A distinct acquisition for reference purposes to the shelf of any practitioner."—*Law Notes.*

16 STEVENS & HAYNES, BELL YARD, TEMPLE BAR.

Third Edition, in one vol., price 20s., cloth,

A COMPENDIUM OF THE LAW OF PROPERTY IN LAND.

FOR THE USE OF STUDENTS AND THE PROFESSION.

THIRD EDITION WITH ADDENDA, GIVING THE LAND TRANSFER ACT, 1897, WITH REFERENCES TO THE TEXT.

BY WILLIAM DOUGLAS EDWARDS, LL.B.,

OF LINCOLN'S INN, BARRISTER-AT-LAW.

"Mr. Edwards' treatise on the Law of Real Property is marked by excellency of arrangement and conciseness of statement. . . . . We are glad to see, by the appearance of successive editions, that the merits of the book are appreciated."—*Solicitors' Journal.*

"So excellent is the arrangement that we know of no better compendium upon the subject of which it treats."—*Law Times.*

"We welcome the third edition of Mr. Edwards' book. It has by this time secured a first place amongst students' books on Real Property, both by its admirable arrangement of topics and by the clearness of its statements. The present edition incorporates the Statutes and Cases for 1896."—*Cambridge Review.*

"An established place in legal literature is occupied by Mr. W. D. Edwards' 'Compendium of the Law of Property in Land,' the third edition of which has just been published."—*The Globe.*

"We consider it one of the best works published on Real Property Law."—*Law Students' Journal.*

"Another excellent compendium which has entered a second edition is Mr. Edwards' 'Compendium of the Law of Property in Land.' No work on English law is written more perspicuously."—*Law Times.*

"The author has the merit of being a sound lawyer, a merit perhaps not always possessed by the authors of legal text-books for students."—*Law Quarterly Review.*

"Altogether it is a work for which we are indebted to the author, and is worthy of the improved notions of law which the study of jurisprudence is bringing to the front."—*Solicitors' Journal.*

Third Edition, royal 8vo, price 38s., cloth,

THE

LAW OF CORPORATIONS AND COMPANIES.

A TREATISE ON THE DOCTRINE OF

ULTRA VIRES:

BEING

An Investigation of the Principles which Limit the Capacities, Powers, and Liabilities of

CORPORATIONS,

AND MORE ESPECIALLY OF

JOINT STOCK COMPANIES.

By SEWARD BRICE, M.A., LL.D., LONDON,

OF THE INNER TEMPLE, ONE OF HER MAJESTY'S COUNSEL.

THIRD EDITION.

REVISED THROUGHOUT AND ENLARGED, AND CONTAINING THE UNITED STATES AND COLONIAL DECISIONS.

REVIEWS.

". . . . On the whole, we consider Mr. Brice's exhaustive work a valuable addition to the literature of the profession."—SATURDAY REVIEW.

"It is the Law of Corporations that Mr. Brice treats of (and treats of more fully, and at the same time more scientifically, than any work with which we are acquainted), not the law of principal and agent; and Mr. Brice does not do his book justice by giving it so vague a title."—*Law Journal.*

"On this doctrine, first introduced in the Common Law Courts in *East Anglian Railway Co.* v. *Eastern Counties Railway Co.*, BRICE ON ULTRA VIRES may be read with advantage."—*Judgment of* LORD JUSTICE BRAMWELL, *in the Case of Evershed* v. *L. & N. W. Ry. Co.* (L. R., 3 Q. B. Div. 141.).

Seventh Edition, in royal 8vo, price 36s., cloth,

BUCKLEY ON THE COMPANIES ACTS.

THE LAW AND PRACTICE UNDER THE COMPANIES ACTS, 1862 TO 1893; AND THE LIFE ASSURANCE COMPANIES ACTS, 1870 TO 1872; INCLUDING THE COMPANIES (MEMORANDUM OF ASSOCIATION) ACT; THE COMPANIES (WINDING-UP) ACT, AND THE DIRECTORS' LIABILITY ACT.

A Treatise on the Law of Joint Stock Companies.

CONTAINING THE STATUTES, WITH THE RULES, ORDERS, AND FORMS, TO REGULATE PROCEEDINGS.

SEVENTH EDITION BY THE AUTHOR, and
A. C. CLAUSON, *Esq.*, *M.A.*,
OF LINCOLN'S INN, BARRISTER-AT-LAW.

Second Edition, with Supplement, in royal 8vo, price 46s., cloth.

THE LAW RELATING TO

SHIPMASTERS AND SEAMEN.

THEIR APPOINTMENT, DUTIES, POWERS, RIGHTS, LIABILITIES AND REMEDIES.

BY THE LATE JOSEPH KAY, ESQ., M.A., Q.C.

Second Edition.

WITH A SUPPLEMENT

Comprising THE MERCHANT SHIPPING ACT, 1894, *The Rules of Court made thereunder, and the (proposed) Regulations for Preventing Collisions at Sea.*

BY THE HON. J. W. MANSFIELD, M.A., AND
G. W. DUNCAN, ESQ., B.A.,
OF THE INNER TEMPLE, BARRISTERS-AT-LAW.

REVIEWS OF THE SECOND EDITION:

"It will, however, be a valuable book of reference for any lawyer desiring to look up a point connected with the rights and duties of a shipmaster or a seaman—the list of cases cited covers nearly seventy pages—while any shipmaster, shipagent or consul who masters this edition will be well posted up. . . . . We hope this new Edition will be quickly appreciated, for the

Editors have carried out an arduous task carefully and well."—*Law Journal*, April, 1894.

"It has had practical and expert knowledge brought to bear upon it, while the case law is brought down to a very late date. Considerable improvement has been made in the index."—*Law Times*, April, 1894.

In royal 8vo, price 10s. 6d., cloth,

THE MERCHANT SHIPPING ACT, 1894:

With the Rules of Court made thereunder. Being a Supplement to KAY'S LAW RELATING TO SHIPMASTERS AND SEAMEN. To which are added the (proposed) Regulations for Preventing Collisions at Sea. With Notes. By Hon. J. W. MANSFIELD, M.A., and G. W. DUNCAN, B.A., of the Inner Temple, Barristers-at-Law.

18 STEVENS & HAYNES, BELL YARD, TEMPLE BAR.

Fourth Edition, in royal 8vo, price 40s., cloth,

THE JUDGMENTS, ORDERS, AND PRACTICE OF THE SUPREME COURT,

CHIEFLY in RESPECT to ACTIONS ASSIGNED to the CHANCERY DIVISION.

By LOFTUS LEIGH PEMBERTON,

One of the registrars of the Supreme Court of Judicature ; and Author of " The Practice in Equity by way of Revivor and Supplement."

"The work under notice ought to be of considerable service to the profession. . . . . . The forms throughout the work—and they are the most important element in it—appear to us to be accurate, and of the most approved type. This fact alone will commend the new edition to practitioners in the Chancery Division. There is a useful table of the Lord Chancellors and Judges at the beginning of the book, and a very full index concludes it."—*Law Times.*

In demy 12mo, price 5s.,

THE STATUTORY LAW RELATING TO TRUSTEE SAVINGS BANKS (1863—1891),

together with the Treasury Regulations (1888—1889), and the Scheme for the Appointment of the Inspection Committee of Trustee Savings Banks. By URQUHART A. FORBES, of Lincoln's Inn, Esq., Barrister-at-Law, Author of "The Law Relating to Savings Banks ;" the "Law of Savings Banks since 1878 ;" and joint Author of "The Law Relating to Water."

In demy 12mo, price 6s., cloth,

THE LAW OF SAVINGS BANKS SINCE 1878;

With a Digest of Decisions made by the Chief Registrar and Assistant Registrars of Friendly Societies from 1878 to 1882, being a Supplement to the Law relating to Trustee and Post Office Savings Banks.

By U. A. FORBES, of Lincoln's Inn, Barrister-at-Law.

⁎ *The complete work can be had, price* 10s. 6d., *cloth.*

In 8vo, price 15s., cloth,

THE LAW AND PRACTICE RELATING TO

THE ADMINISTRATION OF DECEASED PERSONS

BY THE CHANCERY DIVISION OF THE HIGH COURT OF JUSTICE;

WITH AN ADDENDA giving the alterations effected by the NEW RULES of 1883, AND AN APPENDIX OF ORDERS AND FORMS, ANNOTATED BY REFERENCES TO THE TEXT.

By W. GREGORY WALKER and EDGAR J. ELGOOD,

OF LINCOLN'S INN, BARRISTERS-AT-LAW.

" In this volume the most important branch of the administrative business of the Chancery Division is treated with conciseness and care. Judging from the admirable clearness of expression which characterises the entire work, and the labour which has evidently been bestowed on every detail, we do not think that a literary executorship could have devolved upon a more able and conscientious representative . . . . Useful chapters are introduced in their appropriate places, dealing with the ' Parties to administration actions,' ' The proofs of claims in Chambers,' and ' The cost of administration actions.' To the last-mentioned chapter we gladly accord special praise, as a clear and succinct summary of the law, from which, so far as we have tested it, no proposition of any importance has been omitted . . . . An elaborately constructed table of cases, with references in separate columns to all the reports, and a fairly good index, much increase the utility of the work."—*Solicitors' Journal.*

In Foolscap 8vo, superfine paper, bound in Vellum, price 3s. 6d. net.

⁎ *A limited number of copies have been printed upon large paper, price* 7s. 6d. *net.*

SCINTILLAE JURIS.

CHARLES J. DARLING, Q.C., M.P. With a Frontispiece and Colophon by FRANK LOCKWOOD, Q.C., M.P. Fourth Edition (Enlarged).

"'Scintillae Juris' is that little bundle of humorous essays on law and cognate matters which, since the day of its first appearance, some years ago, has been the delight of legal circles. . . . It has a quality of style which suggests much study of Bacon in his lighter vein. Its best essays would not be unworthy of the Essays, and if read out, one by one, before a blindfolded *connoisseur*, might often be assigned to that wonderful book."—*Daily News.*

Second Edition, in 8vo, price 25s., cloth,

THE PRINCIPLES OF
THE LAW OF RATING OF HEREDITAMENTS
IN THE OCCUPATION OF COMPANIES.
By J. H. BALFOUR BROWNE,
OF THE MIDDLE TEMPLE, Q.C.,
And D. N. McNAUGHTON, of the Middle Temple, Barrister-at-Law.

"The tables and specimen valuations which are printed in an appendix to this volume will be of great service to the parish authorities, and to the legal practitioners who may have to deal with the rating of those properties which are in the occupation of Companies, and we congratulate Mr. Browne on the production of a clear and concise book of the system of Company Rating. There is no doubt that such a work is much needed, and we are sure that all those who are interested in, or have to do with, public rating, will find it of great service. Much credit is therefore due to Mr. Browne for his able treatise—a work which his experience as Registrar of the Railway Commission peculiarly qualified him to undertake."—*Law Magazine.*

In 8vo, 1875, price 7s. 6d., cloth,

THE LAW OF USAGES & CUSTOMS:
A Practical Law Tract.
By J. H. BALFOUR BROWNE,
OF THE MIDDLE TEMPLE, Q.C.

"We look upon this treatise as a valuable addition to works written on the Science of Law."—*Canada Law Journal.*

"As a tract upon a very troublesome department of Law it is admirable—the principles laid down are sound, the illustrations are well chosen, and the decisions and *dicta* are harmonised so far as possible and distinguished when necessary."—*Irish Law Times.*

"As a book of reference we know of none so comprehensive dealing with this particular branch of Common Law. . . . In this way the book is invaluable to the practitioner."—*Law Magazine.*

In one volume, 8vo, 1875, price 18s., cloth,

THE PRACTICE BEFORE THE RAILWAY COMMISSIONERS
UNDER THE REGULATION OF RAILWAY ACTS, 1873 & 1874;
With the Amended General Orders of the Commissioners, Schedule of Forms, and Table of Fees; together with the Law of Undue Preference, the Law of the Jurisdiction of the Railway Commissioners, Notes of their Decisions and Orders, Precedents of Forms of Applications, Answers and Replies, and Appendices of Statutes and Cases.
By J. H. BALFOUR BROWNE,
OF THE MIDDLE TEMPLE, Q.C.

"Mr. Browne's book is handy and convenient in form, and well arranged for the purpose of reference: its treatment of the subject is fully and carefully worked out: it is, so far as we have been able to test it, accurate and trustworthy. It is the work of a man of capable legal attainments, and by official position intimate with his subject; and we therefore think that it cannot fail to meet a real want and to prove of service to the legal profession and the public."—*Law Magazine.*

In 8vo, 1876, price 7s. 6d., cloth,

ON THE COMPULSORY PURCHASE OF THE UNDERTAKINGS OF COMPANIES BY CORPORATIONS,
And the Practice in Relation to the Passage of Bills for Compulsory Purchase through Parliament. By J. H. BALFOUR BROWNE, of the Middle Temple, Q.C.

"This is a work of considerable importance to all Municipal Corporations, and it is hardly too much to say that every member of these bodies should have a copy by him for constant reference. Probably at no very distant date the property of all the existing gas and water companies will pass under municipal control, and therefore it is exceedingly desirable that the principles and conditions under which such transfers ought to be made should be clearly understood. This task is made easy by the present volume. The stimulus for the publication of such a work was given by the action of the 'Parliamentary Committee which last session passed the preamble of the 'Stockton and Middlesborough Corporations Water Bill, 1876.' The volume accordingly contains a full report of the case as it was presented both by the promoters and opponents, and as his was the first time in which the principle of compulsory purchase was definitely recognised, there can be no doubt that it will long be regarded as a leading case. As a matter of course, many incidental points of interest arose during the progress of the case. Thus, besides the main question of compulsory purchase, and the question as to whether there was or was not any precedent for the Bill, the questions of water compensations, of appeals from one Committee to another, and other kindred subjects were discussed. These are all treated at length by the Author in the body of the work, which is thus a complete legal compendium on the large subject with which it so ably deals."

20　STEVENS & HAYNES, BELL YARD, TEMPLE BAR.

Second Edition, in crown 8vo, price 12s. 6d., cloth.

THE LAW OF EVIDENCE,

By S. L. PHIPSON, M.A., of the Inner Temple, Barrister-at-Law.

"This book condenses a head of law into a comparatively small compass—a class of literary undertaking to which every encouragement should be given. . . . The volume is most portable, most compendious, and as far as we have been able to examine it, as accurate as any law book can be expected to be."—*Law Times.*

"We are of opinion that Mr. Phipson has produced a book which will be found very serviceable, not only for practitioners, but also for students. We have tried it in a good many places, and we find that it is well brought down to date."—*Law Journal.*

In 8vo, price 5s., cloth,

THEORIES AND CRITICISMS OF SIR HENRY MAINE.

By MORGAN O. EVANS, Barrister-at-Law.

Contained in his six works, "Ancient Law," "Early Law and Customs," "Early History of Institutions," "Village Communities," "International Law," and "Popular Government," which works have to be studied for the various examinations.

In 8vo, 1872, price 7s. 6d., cloth,

AN EPITOME AND ANALYSIS OF

SAVIGNY'S TREATISE ON OBLIGATIONS IN ROMAN LAW.

By ARCHIBALD BROWN, M.A.

EDIN. AND OXON., AND B.C.L. OXON., OF THE MIDDLE TEMPLE, BARRISTER-AT-LAW.

"Mr. Archibald Brown deserves the thanks of all interested in the science of Law, whether as a study or a practice, for his edition of Herr von Savigny's great work on 'Obligations.' Mr. Brown has undertaken a double task—the translation of his author, and the analysis of his author's matter. That he has succeeded in reducing the bulk of the original will be seen at a glance ;
the French translation consisting of two volumes, with some five hundred pages apiece, as compared with Mr. Brown's thin volume of a hundred and fifty pages. At the same time the pith of Von Savigny's matter seems to be very successfully preserved, nothing which might be useful to the English reader being apparently omitted."—*Law Journal.*

THE ELEMENTS OF ROMAN LAW.

Second Edition, in crown 8vo, price 6s., cloth,

A CONCISE DIGEST OF THE

INSTITUTES OF GAIUS AND JUSTINIAN.

With copious References arranged in Parallel Columns, also Chronological and Analytical Tables, Lists of Laws, &c. &c.

Primarily designed for the Use of Students preparing for Examination at Oxford, Cambridge, and the Inns of Court.

By SEYMOUR F. HARRIS, B.C.L., M.A.,

WORCESTER COLLEGE, OXFORD, AND THE INNER TEMPLE, BARRISTER-AT-LAW;
AUTHOR OF "UNIVERSITIES AND LEGAL EDUCATION."

"Mr. Harris's digest ought to have very great success among law students both in the Inns of Court and the Universities. His book gives evidence of praiseworthy accuracy and laborious condensation."—LAW JOURNAL.

"This book contains a summary in English of the elements of Roman Law as contained in the works of Gaius and Justinian, and is so arranged that the reader can at once see what are the opinions of either of these two writers on each point. From the very exact and accurate references to titles and sections given he can at once refer to the original writers. The concise manner in which Mr. Harris has arranged his digest will render it most useful, not only to the students for whom it was originally written, but also to those persons who, though they may have no time to wade through the larger treatises of Poste, Sanders, Ortolan, and others, yet desire to obtain some knowledge of Roman Law."—OXFORD AND CAMBRIDGE UNDERGRADUATES' JOURNAL.

"Mr. Harris deserves the credit of having produced an epitome which will be of service to those numerous students who have no time or sufficient ability to analyse the Institutes for themselves."—LAW TIMES.

WORKS FOR LAW STUDENTS.

Fifth Edition, in crown 8vo, price 15s., cloth,

ENGLISH CONSTITUTIONAL HISTORY:
FROM THE TEUTONIC INVASION TO THE PRESENT TIME.

Designed as a Text-book for Students and others,

By T. P. TASWELL-LANGMEAD, B.C.L.,

OF LINCOLN'S INN, BARRISTER-AT-LAW, FORMERLY VINERIAN SCHOLAR IN THE UNIVERSITY
AND LATE PROFESSOR OF CONSTITUTIONAL LAW AND HISTORY,
UNIVERSITY COLLEGE, LONDON.

Fifth Edition, Revised throughout, with Notes,

By PHILIP A. ASHWORTH,

BARRISTER-AT-LAW; TRANSLATOR OF GNEIST'S "HISTORY OF THE ENGLISH CONSTITUTION."

"We heartily commend this valuable book to the study of all, whether Conservative or Liberal in politics, who desire to take an intelligent part in public life."—*The New Saturday.*
"'Taswell-Langmead' has long been popular with candidates for examination in Constitutional History, and the present edition should render it even more so. It is now, in our opinion, the ideal students' book upon the subject."—*Law Notes.*
"Mr. Carmichael has performed his allotted task with credit to himself, and the high standard of excellence attained by Taswell-Langmead's treatise is worthily maintained. This, the third edition, will be found as useful as its predecessors to the large class of readers and students who seek in its pages accurate knowledge of the history of the constitution."—*Law Times.*
"To the student of constitutional law this work will be invaluable. . . . . The book is remarkable for the raciness and vigour of its style. The editorial contributions of Mr. Carmichael are judicious, and add much to the value of the work."—*Scottish Law Review.*
"The work will continue to hold the field as the best class-book on the subject."—*Contemporary Review.*
"The book is well known as an admirable introduction to the study of constitutional law for students at law. . . . . Mr. Carmichael appears to have done the work of editing, made necessary by the death of Mr. Taswell-Langmead, with care and judgment."—*Law Journal.*
"The work before us it would be hardly possible to praise too highly. In style, arrangement, clearness, and size, it would be difficult to find anything better on the real history of England, the history of its constitutional growth as a complete story, than this volume."—*Boston (U.S.) Literary World.*
"As it now stands, we should find it hard to name a better text-book on English Constitutional History."—*Solicitors' Journal.*
"Mr. Taswell-Langmead's compendium of the rise and development of the English Constitution has evidently supplied a want. . . . The present Edition is greatly improved. . . . We have no hesitation in saying that it is a thoroughly good and useful work."—*Spectator.*
"It is a safe, careful, praiseworthy digest and manual of all constitutional history and law."—*Globe.*
"The volume on English Constitutional History, by Mr. Taswell-Langmead, is exactly what such a history should be."—*Standard.*
"Mr. Taswell-Langmead has thoroughly grasped the bearings of his subject. It is, however, in dealing with that chief subject of constitutional history—parliamentary government—that the work exhibits its great superiority over its rivals."—*Academy.*

Second Edition, in 8vo, price 6s., cloth,

HANDBOOK TO THE INTERMEDIATE AND FINAL LL.B. OF LONDON UNIVERSITY;
(PASS AND HONOURS).

INCLUDING A COMPLETE SUMMARY OF "AUSTIN'S JURISPRUDENCE," AND THE EXAMINATION PAPERS OF LATE YEARS IN ALL BRANCHES.

By a B.A., LL.B. (Lond.).

In crown 8vo, price 3s.; or Interleaved for Notes, price 4s.,

CONTRACT LAW.

QUESTIONS ON THE LAW OF CONTRACTS. WITH NOTES TO THE ANSWERS. *Founded on* "*Anson*," "*Chitty*," *and* "*Pollock.*"

By PHILIP FOSTER ALDRED, D.C.L., Hertford College and Gray's Inn.

WORKS FOR LAW STUDENTS.

Twelfth Edition, in 8vo, price 21s., cloth,

THE PRINCIPLES OF EQUITY

INTENDED FOR THE USE OF STUDENTS AND THE PROFESSION.

By EDMUND H. T. SNELL,
OF THE MIDDLE TEMPLE, BARRISTER-AT-LAW.

TWELFTH EDITION.

By ARCHIBALD BROWN, M.A. EDIN. & OXON., & B.C.L. OXON.,
OF THE MIDDLE TEMPLE, BARRISTER-AT-LAW; AUTHOR OF "A NEW LAW DICTIONARY," "AN ANALYSIS OF SAVIGNY ON OBLIGATIONS," AND THE "LAW OF FIXTURES."

REVIEWS.

"The Eleventh Edition of 'Snell's Equity' is remarkable in one respect, viz., the learned editor has, as he tells us in his preface, actually succeeded in diminishing the size of the book. It is the Eighth Edition which has passed through the able hands of Mr. Archibald Brown, and the deserved reputation of the work has certainly not suffered any loss in the process. In the present edition the book is well brought up to date. ... The printing and get-up of the book are excellent and the index is good."—*Law Journal.*

"This is the Eighth Edition of this student's text-book which the present editor has brought out. ... the book is a good introduction to Equity, and is additionally useful by having a full index."—*Solicitors' Journal.*

"The book remains what it always has been, the indispensable guide to the beginner of the study of Equity, without ceasing to be above the notice of the more experienced student."—*Oxford Magazine.*

"Whether to the beginner in the study of the principles of Equity, or to the practising lawyer in the hurry of work, it can be unhesitatingly recommended as a standard and invaluable treatise."—*Cambridge Review.*

"This work on the 'Principles of Equity' has, since the publication of the First Edition, been recognised as the best elementary treatise on the subject, and it would not be necessary to say more of this Edition, than to mention the fact of its publication, were it not for the fact that the author, Mr. Snell, is dead, and the late Editions have been brought out under the care of Mr. Brown. It seldom happens that a new editor is able to improve on the work of his predecessor in its plan or its details. But in the case of the present work we find that each edition is a manifest improvement on the former ones, and well as Mr. Snell did his work we discover that Mr. Brown has done it better."—*Irish Law Times.*

"This is now unquestionably the standard book on Equity for students."—*Saturday Review.*

"We know of no better introduction to the Principles of Equity."— CANADA LAW JOURNAL.

Sixth Edition, in 8vo, in the Press,

AN ANALYSIS OF SNELL'S PRINCIPLES OF EQUITY. FOUNDED ON THE TWELFTH EDITION. With Notes thereon.
By E. E. BLYTH, LL.D., Solicitor.

"Mr. Blyth's book will undoubtedly be very useful to readers of Snell."—*Law Times.*
"This is an admirable analysis of a good treatise; read with Snell, this little book will be found very profitable to the student."—*Law Journal.*

In 8vo, price 2s., sewed,

QUESTIONS ON EQUITY.
FOR STUDENTS PREPARING FOR EXAMINATION.
FOUNDED ON THE NINTH EDITION OF
SNELL'S "PRINCIPLES OF EQUITY."
By W. T. WAITE,
BARRISTER-AT-LAW, HOLT SCHOLAR OF THE HONOURABLE SOCIETY OF GRAY'S INN.

WORKS FOR LAW STUDENTS.

Second Edition, in one volume, 8vo, price 18s., cloth,

PRINCIPLES OF CONVEYANCING.

AN ELEMENTARY WORK FOR THE USE OF STUDENTS.

By HENRY C. DEANE,

OF LINCOLN'S INN, BARRISTER-AT-LAW, SOMETIME LECTURER TO THE INCORPORATED LAW SOCIETY OF THE UNITED KINGDOM.

"*We hope to see this book, like Snell's Equity, a standard class-book in all Law Schools where English law is taught.*"—CANADA LAW JOURNAL.

"We like the work, it is well written and is an excellent student's book, and being only just published, it has the great advantage of having in it all the recent important enactments relating to conveyancing. It possesses also an excellent index."—*Law Students' Journal.*

"Will be found of great use to students entering upon the difficulties of Real Property Law. It has an unusually exhaustive index covering some fifty pages."—*Law Times.*

"In the parts which have been re-written, Mr. Deane has preserved the same pleasant style marked by simplicity and lucidity which distinguished his first edition. After 'Williams on Real Property,' there is no book which we should so strongly recommend to the student entering upon Real Property Law as Mr. Deane's 'Principles of Conveyancing,' and the high character which the first edition attained has been fully kept up in this second."—*Law Journal.*

Fourth Edition, in 8vo, price 10s., cloth,

A SUMMARY OF THE

LAW & PRACTICE IN ADMIRALTY.

FOR THE USE OF STUDENTS.

By EUSTACE SMITH,

OF THE INNER TEMPLE; AUTHOR OF "A SUMMARY OF COMPANY LAW."

"The book is well arranged, and forms a good introduction to the subject."—*Solicitors' Journal.*

"It is, however, in our opinion, a well and carefully written little work, and should be in the hands of every student who is taking up Admiralty Law at the Final."—*Law Students' Journal.*

"Mr. Smith has a happy knack of compressing a large amount of useful matter in a small compass. The present work will doubtless be received with satisfaction equal to that with which his previous 'Summary' has been met."—*Oxford and Cambridge Undergraduates' Journal.*

Fourth Edition, in 8vo, price 8s., cloth,

A SUMMARY OF THE

LAW AND PRACTICE IN THE ECCLESIASTICAL COURTS.

FOR THE USE OF STUDENTS.

By EUSTACE SMITH,

THE INNER TEMPLE; AUTHOR OF "A SUMMARY OF COMPANY LAW," AND "A SUMMARY OF THE LAW AND PRACTICE IN ADMIRALTY."

"His object has been, as he tells us in his preface, to give the student and general reader a fair outline of the scope and extent of ecclesiastical law, of the principles on which it is founded, of the Courts by which it is enforced, and the procedure by which these Courts are regulated. We think the book well fulfils its object. Its value is much enhanced by a profuse citation of authorities for the propositions contained in it."—*Bar Examination Journal.*

Fourth Edition, in 8vo, price 7s. 6d., cloth,

AN EPITOME OF THE LAWS OF PROBATE AND DIVORCE.

FOR THE USE OF STUDENTS FOR HONOURS EXAMINATION.

By J. CARTER HARRISON, SOLICITOR.

"The work is considerably enlarged, and we think improved, and will be found of great assistance to students."—*Law Students' Journal.*

Eighth Edition. In one volume, 8vo., in the Press.

PRINCIPLES OF THE COMMON LAW.

INTENDED FOR THE USE OF STUDENTS AND THE PROFESSION.

EIGHTH EDITION.

By JOHN INDERMAUR, SOLICITOR,

AUTHOR OF "A MANUAL OF THE PRACTICE OF THE SUPREME COURT,"
"EPITOMES OF LEADING CASES," AND OTHER WORKS.

"The student will find in Mr. Indermaur's book a safe and clear guide to the Principles of Common Law."—*Law Journal,* 1892.

"The present edition of this elementary treatise has been in general edited with praiseworthy care. The provisions of the statutes affecting the subjects discussed, which have been passed since the publication of the last edition, are clearly summarised, and the effect of the leading cases is generally very well given. In the difficult task of selecting and distinguishing principle from detail, Mr. Indermaur has been very successful; the leading principles are clearly brought out, and very judiciously illustrated."—*Solicitors' Journal.*

"The work is acknowledged to be one of the best written and most useful elementary works for Law Students that has been published."—*Law Times.*

"The praise which we were enabled to bestow upon Mr. Indermaur's very useful compilation on its first appearance has been justified by a demand for a second edition."—*Law Magazine.*

"We were able, four years ago, to praise the first edition of Mr. Indermaur's book as likely to be of use to students in acquiring the elements of the law of torts and contracts. The second edition maintains the character of the book."—*Law Journal.*

"Mr. Indermaur renders even law light reading. He not only possesses the faculty of judicious selection, but of lucid exposition and felicitous illustration. And while his works are all thus characterised, his 'Principles of the Common Law' especially displays those features. That it has already reached a second edition, testifies that our estimate of the work on its first appearance was not unduly favourable, highly as we then signified approval; nor needs it that we should add anything to that estimate in reference to the general scope and execution of the work. It only remains to say, that the present edition evinces that every care has been taken to insure thorough accuracy, while including all the modifications in the law that have taken place since the original publication; and that the references to the Irish decisions which have been now introduced are calculated to render the work of greater utility to practitioners and students, *both* English and Irish."
—*Irish Law Times.*

"*This work, the author tells us in his Preface, is written mainly with a view to the examinations of the Incorporated Law Society; but we think it is likely to attain a wider usefulness. It seems, so far as we can judge from the parts we have examined, to be a careful and clear outline of the principles of the common law. It is very readable; and not only students, but many practitioners and the public might benefit by a perusal of its pages.*"—SOLICITORS' JOURNAL.

WORKS FOR LAW STUDENTS. 25

Seventh Edition, in 8vo, price 14s., cloth,

A MANUAL OF THE PRACTICE OF THE SUPREME COURT OF JUDICATURE,
IN THE QUEEN'S BENCH AND CHANCERY DIVISIONS.
Seventh Edition.
Intended for the use of Students and the Profession.
By JOHN INDERMAUR, Solicitor.

"Mr. Indermaur has brought out a sixth edition of his excellent 'Manual of Practice' at a very opportune time, for he has been able to incorporate the effect of the new Rules of Court which came into force last November, the Trustee Act, 1893, and Rules, and the Supreme Court Fund Rules, 1893, as well as that of other Acts of earlier date. A very complete revision of the work has, of course, been necessary, and Mr. Indermaur, assisted by Mr. Thwaites, has effected this with his usual thoroughness and careful attention to details. "The book is well known and valued by students, but practitioners also find it handy in many cases where reference to the bulkier 'White Book' is unnecessary."—*Law Times, February*, 1894.

"This well-known students' book may very well be consulted by practitioners, as it contains a considerable amount of reliable information on the practice of the Court. It is written so as to include the new Rules, and a supplemental note deals with the alterations made in Rule XI. by the Judges in January last. The praise which we gave to previous editions is quite due to the present issue."—*Law Journal, February*, 1894.

Eighth Edition, in 8vo, price 6s., cloth,

AN EPITOME OF LEADING COMMON LAW CASES;
WITH SOME SHORT NOTES THEREON.
Chiefly intended as a Guide to "SMITH'S LEADING CASES." By JOHN INDERMAUR, Solicitor (Clifford's Inn Prizeman, Michaelmas Term, 1872).

"We have received the third edition of the 'Epitome of Leading Common Law Cases,' by Mr. Indermaur, Solicitor. The first edition of this work was published in February, 1873, the second in April, 1874; and now we have a third edition dated September, 1875. No better proof of the value of this book can be furnished than the fact that in less than three years it has reached a third edition."—*Law Journal*.

Eighth Edition, in 8vo, price 6s., cloth,

AN EPITOME OF LEADING CONVEYANCING AND EQUITY CASES;
WITH SOME SHORT NOTES THEREON, FOR THE USE OF STUDENTS.
By JOHN INDERMAUR, Solicitor, Author of "An Epitome of Leading Common Law Cases."

"We have received the second edition of Mr. Indermaur's very useful Epitome of Leading Conveyancing and Equity Cases. The work is very well done."—*Law Times*.
"The Epitome well deserves the continued patronage of the class—Students—for whom it is especially intended. Mr. Indermaur will soon be known as the 'Students' Friend.'"—*Canada Law Journal*.

Sixth Edition, 8vo, price 6s., cloth,

THE ARTICLED CLERK'S GUIDE TO AND SELF-PREPARATION FOR THE FINAL EXAMINATION.
Containing a Complete Course of Study, with Books to Read, List of Statutes, Cases, Test Questions, &c., and intended for the use of those Articled Clerks who read by themselves. By JOHN INDERMAUR, Solicitor.

"In this edition Mr. Indermaur extends his counsels to the whole period from the Intermediate examination to the Final. His advice is practical and sensible: and if the course of study he recommends is intelligently followed, the articled clerk will have laid in a store of legal knowledge more than sufficient to carry him through the Final Examination."—*Solicitors' Journal*.

Now ready, Fifth Edition, in 8vo, price 10s., cloth,

THE ARTICLED CLERK'S GUIDE TO AND SELF-PREPARATION FOR THE INTERMEDIATE EXAMINATION,
As it now exists on Stephen's Commentaries. Containing a complete course of Study, with Statutes, Questions, and Advice. Also a complete Selected Digest of the whole of the Questions and Answers set at the Examinations on those parts of "Stephen" now examined on, embracing a period of fourteen and a half years (58 Examinations), inclusive of the Examination in April, 1894, &c. &c., and intended for the use of all Articled Clerks who have not yet passed the Intermediate Examination. By JOHN INDERMAUR, Author of "Principles of Common Law," and other works.

In 8vo, 1875, price 6s., cloth,

THE STUDENTS' GUIDE TO THE JUDICATURE ACTS,
AND THE RULES THEREUNDER:
Being a book of Questions and Answers intended for the use of Law Students.
By JOHN INDERMAUR, Solicitor.

WORKS FOR LAW STUDENTS.

Fifth Edition, in crown 8vo, price 12s. 6d., cloth,

AN EPITOME OF CONVEYANCING STATUTES,

EXTENDING FROM 13 EDW. I. TO THE END OF 55 & 56 VICTORIÆ. Fifth Edition, with Short Notes. By GEORGE NICHOLS MARCY, of Lincoln's Inn, Barrister-at-Law.

Second Edition, in 8vo,

A NEW LAW DICTIONARY,

AND INSTITUTE OF THE WHOLE LAW;

EMBRACING FRENCH AND LATIN TERMS AND REFERENCES TO THE AUTHORITIES, CASES, AND STATUTES.

SECOND EDITION, revised throughout, and considerably enlarged.

By ARCHIBALD BROWN,

M.A. EDIN. AND OXON., AND B.C.L. OXON., OF THE MIDDLE TEMPLE, BARRISTER-AT-LAW; AUTHOR OF THE "LAW OF FIXTURES," "ANALYSIS OF SAVIGNY'S OBLIGATIONS IN ROMAN LAW," ETC.

Reviews of the Second Edition.

"*So far as we have been able to examine the work, it seems to have been most carefully and accurately executed, the present Edition, besides containing much new matter, having been thoroughly revised in consequence of the recent changes in the law; and we have no doubt whatever that it will be found extremely useful, not only to students and practitioners, but to public men, and men of letters.*"—IRISH LAW TIMES.

"*Mr. Brown has revised his Dictionary, and adapted it to the changes effected by the Judicature Acts, and it now constitutes a very useful work to put into the hands of any student or articled clerk, and a work which the practitioner will find of value for reference.*"—SOLICITORS' JOURNAL.

"*It will prove a reliable guide to law students, and a handy book of reference for practitioners.*"—LAW TIMES.

In royal 8vo, price 5s., cloth,

ANALYTICAL TABLES

OF

THE LAW OF REAL PROPERTY;

Drawn up chiefly from STEPHEN'S BLACKSTONE, with Notes.

By C. J. TARRING, of the Inner Temple, Barrister-at-Law.

CONTENTS.

TABLE	I. Tenures.	TABLE	V. Uses.
,,	II. Estates, according to quantity of Tenants' Interest.	,,	VI. Acquisition of Estates in land of freehold tenure.
,,	III. Estates, according to the time at which the Interest is to be enjoyed.	,,	VII. Incorporeal Hereditaments.
,,	IV. Estates, according to the number and connection of the Tenants.	,,	VIII. Incorporeal Hereditaments.

"Great care and considerable skill have been shown in the compilation of these tables, which will be found of much service to students of the Law of Real Property."—*Law Times.*

WORKS FOR LAW STUDENTS.

Seventh Edition, in 8vo, price 20s., cloth,

PRINCIPLES OF THE CRIMINAL LAW.

INTENDED AS A LUCID EXPOSITION OF THE SUBJECT FOR THE USE OF STUDENTS AND THE PROFESSION.

By SEYMOUR F. HARRIS, B.C.L., M.A. (OXON.),

AUTHOR OF "A CONCISE DIGEST OF THE INSTITUTES OF GAIUS AND JUSTINIAN."

SEVENTH EDITION.

By C. L. ATTENBOROUGH, of the Inner Temple, Barrister-at-Law.

REVIEWS.

"Messrs. Stevens & Haynes have just issued the Seventh Edition of their well known text-book, 'Harris's Principles of the Criminal Law.' For the present edition Mr. Charles L. Attenborough, of the Inner Temple, Barrister-at-Law, is responsible. He has brought the work up to date, and ensured for it a further career of usefulness as the leading student's text-book upon the Criminal Law."—*Law Times.*

"This work is pretty well known as, one designed for the student who is preparing for examination, and for the help of young practitioners. Among articled clerks it has long enjoyed a popularity which is not likely to be interfered with. . . . We have been carefully through the new edition and can cordially commend it."—*Law Student's Journal.*

"The book must be good, and must meet a demand, and Harris's Criminal Law remains as it has always been, an excellent work for obtaining that kind of theoretical knowledge of the criminal law which is so useful at the University Examinations of Oxford and Cambridge."—*Law Notes.*

"The characteristic of the present Edition is the restoration to the book of the character of 'a concise exposition' proclaimed by the title-page. Mr. Attenborough has carefully pruned away the excrescences which had arisen in successive editions, and has improved the work both as regards terseness and clearness of exposition. In both respects it is now an excellent student's book. The text is very well broken up into headings and paragraphs, with short marginal notes—the importance of which, for the convenience of the student, is too often overlooked."—*Solicitors' Journal.*

"*The favourable opinion we expressed of the first edition of this work appears to have been justified by the reception it has met with. Looking through this new Edition, we see no reason to modify the praise we bestowed on the former Edition. The recent cases have been added and the provisions of the Summary Jurisdiction Act are noticed in the chapter relating to Summary Convictions. The book is one of the best manuals of Criminal Law for the student.*"—SOLICITORS' JOURNAL.

"*There is no lack of Works on Criminal Law, but there was room for such a useful handbook of Principles as Mr. Seymour Harris has supplied. Accustomed, by his previous labours, to the task of analysing the law, Mr. Harris has brought to bear upon his present work qualifications well adapted to secure the successful accomplishment of the object which he had set before him. That object is not an ambitious one, for it does not pretend to soar above utility to the young practitioner and the student. For both these classes, and for the yet wider class who may require a book of reference on the subject, Mr. Harris has produced a clear and convenient Epitome of the Law.*"—LAW MAGAZINE AND REVIEW.

"This work purports to contain 'a concise exposition of the nature of crime, the various offences punishable by the English law, the law of criminal procedure, and the law of summary convictions,' with tables of offences, punishments, and statutes. The work is divided into four books. Book I. treats of crime, its divisions and essentials; of persons capable of committing crimes; and of principals and accessories. Book II. deals with offences of a public nature; offences against private persons; and offences against the property of individuals. Each crime is discussed in its turn, with as much brevity as could well be used consistently with a proper explanation of the legal characteristics of the several offences. Book III. explains criminal procedure, including the jurisdiction of Courts, and the various steps in the apprehension and trial of criminals from arrest to punishment. This part of the work is extremely well done, the description of the trial being excellent, and thoroughly calculated to impress the mind of the uninitiated. Book IV. contains a short sketch of 'summary convictions before magistrates out of quarter sessions.' The table of offences at the end of the volume is most useful, and there is a very full index. Altogether we must congratulate Mr. Harris on his adventure."—*Law Journal.*

WORKS FOR LAW STUDENTS.

Second Edition, in crown 8vo, price 5s. 6d., cloth,

THE STUDENTS' GUIDE TO BANKRUPTCY;

Being a Complete Digest of the Law of Bankruptcy in the shape of Questions and Answers, and comprising all Questions asked at the Solicitors' Final Examinations in Bankruptcy since the Bankruptcy Act, 1883, and all important Decisions since that Act. By JOHN INDERMAUR, Solicitor, Author of "Principles of Common Law," &c. &c.

In 12mo, price 5s. 6d., cloth,

A CONCISE TREATISE ON THE LAW OF BILLS OF SALE,

FOR THE USE OF LAWYERS, LAW STUDENTS, AND THE PUBLIC.

Embracing the Acts of 1878 and 1882. Part I.—Of Bills of Sale generally. Part II.—Of the Execution, Attestation, and Registration of Bills of Sale and satisfaction thereof. Part III.—Of the Effects of Bills of Sale as against Creditors. Part IV.—Of Seizing under, and Enforcing Bills of Sale. Appendix, Forms, Acts, &c. By JOHN INDERMAUR, Solicitor.

"The object of the book is thoroughly practical. Those who want to be told exactly what to do and where to go when they are registering a bill of sale will find the necessary information in this little book."
—*Law Journal.*

Second Edition, in 8vo, price 4s., cloth,

A COLLECTION OF LATIN MAXIMS & PHRASES.
LITERALLY TRANSLATED.
INTENDED FOR THE USE OF STUDENTS FOR ALL LEGAL EXAMINATIONS.

Second Edition, by J. N. COTTERELL, Solicitor.

"The book seems admirably adapted as a book of reference for students who come across a Latin maxim in their reading."—*Law Journal.*

In one volume, 8vo, price 9s., cloth,

LEADING STATUTES SUMMARISED,
FOR THE USE OF STUDENTS.

By ERNEST C. THOMAS,

BACON SCHOLAR OF THE HON. SOCIETY OF GRAY'S INN, LATE SCHOLAR OF TRINITY COLLEGE, OXFORD; AUTHOR OF "LEADING CASES IN CONSTITUTIONAL LAW BRIEFLY STATED."

Second Edition, in 8vo, enlarged, price 6s., cloth,

LEADING CASES IN CONSTITUTIONAL LAW
BRIEFLY STATED, WITH INTRODUCTION AND NOTES.

By ERNEST C. THOMAS,

BACON SCHOLAR OF THE HON. SOCIETY OF GRAY'S INN, LATE SCHOLAR OF TRINITY COLLEGE, OXFORD.

"Mr. E. C. Thomas has put together in a slim octavo a digest of the principal cases illustrating Constitutional Law, that is to say, all questions as to the rights or authority of the Crown or persons under it, as regards not merely the constitution and structure given to the governing body, but also the mode in which the sovereign power is to be exercised. In an introductory essay Mr. Thomas gives a very clear and intelligent survey of the general functions of the Executive, and the principles by which they are regulated; and then follows a summary of leading cases."—*Saturday Review.*

"Mr. Thomas gives a sensible introduction and a brief epitome of the familiar leading cases."—*Law Times.*

In 8vo, price 8s., cloth,

AN EPITOME OF HINDU LAW CASES. With

Short Notes thereon. And Introductory Chapters on Sources of Law, Marriage, Adoption, Partition, and Succession. By WILLIAM M. P. COGHLAN, Bombay Civil Service, late Judge and Sessions Judge of Tanna.

Second Edition, in crown 8vo, price 12s. 6d., cloth,

THE BANKRUPTCY ACT, 1883,

WITH NOTES OF ALL THE CASES DECIDED UNDER THE ACT;

THE CONSOLIDATED RULES AND FORMS, 1886; THE DEBTORS ACT, 1869, SO FAR AS APPLICABLE TO BANKRUPTCY MATTERS, WITH RULES AND FORMS THEREUNDER; THE BILLS OF SALE ACTS, 1878 AND 1882;

Board of Trade Circulars and Forms, and List of Official Receivers; Scale of Costs, Fees, and Percentages, 1886; Orders of the Bankruptcy Judge of the High Court; and a Copious Index.

BY WILLIAM HAZLITT, ESQ., AND RICHARD RINGWOOD, M.A.,
SENIOR REGISTRAR IN BANKRUPTCY, OF THE MIDDLE TEMPLE, ESQ., BARRISTER-AT-LAW.

Second Edition, by R. RINGWOOD, M.A., Barrister-at-Law.

"This is a very handy edition of the Act and Rules. . . . . . The cross references and marginal references to corresponding provisions of the Act of 1869 are exceedingly useful. . . . . There is a very full Index, and the book is admirably printed."—*Solicitors' Journal.*

Part I., price 7s. 6d., sewed,

LORD WESTBURY'S DECISIONS IN THE EUROPEAN ARBITRATION. Reported by FRANCIS S. REILLY, of Lincoln's Inn, Barrister-at-Law.

Parts I., II., and III., price 25s., sewed,

LORD CAIRNS'S DECISIONS IN THE ALBERT ARBITRATION. Reported by FRANCIS S. REILLY, of Lincoln's Inn, Barrister-at-Law.

Second Edition, in royal 8vo, price 30s., cloth,

A TREATISE ON

THE STATUTES OF ELIZABETH AGAINST FRAUDULENT CONVEYANCES.

THE BILLS OF SALE ACTS 1878 AND 1882 AND THE LAW OF VOLUNTARY DISPOSITIONS OF PROPERTY.

BY THE LATE H. W. MAY, B.A. (Ch. Ch. Oxford).

Second Edition, thoroughly revised and enlarged, by S. WORTHINGTON WORTHINGTON, of the Inner Temple, Barrister-at-Law; Editor of the "Married Women's Property Acts," 5th edition, by the late J. R. GRIFFITH.

"In conclusion, we can heartily recommend this book to our readers, not only to those who are in large practice, and who merely want a classified list of cases, but to those who have both the desire and the leisure to enter upon a systematic study of our law."—*Solicitors' Journal.*

"As Mr. Worthington points out, since Mr. May wrote, the 'Bills of Sale Acts' of 1878 and 1882 have been passed; the 'Married Women's Property Act, 1882' (making settlements by married women void as against creditors in cases in which similar settlements by a man would be void), and the 'Bankruptcy Act, 1883.' These Acts and the decisions upon them have been handled by Mr. Worthington in a manner which shows that he is master of his subject, and not a slavish copyist of sections and head-notes, which is a vicious propensity of many modern compilers of text-books. His Table of Cases (with reference to all the reports), is admirable, and his Index most exhaustive."—*Law Times.*

"The results of the authorities appear to be given well and tersely, and the treatise will, we think, be found a convenient and trustworthy book of reference."—*Law Journal.*

"Mr. Worthington's work appears to have been conscientious and exhaustive."—*Saturday Review.*

"Examining Mr. May's book, we find it constructed with an intelligence and precision which render it entirely worthy of being accepted as a guide in this confessedly difficult subject. The subject is an involved one, but with clean and clear handling it is here presented as clearly as it could be. . . . On the whole, he has produced a very useful book of an exceptionally scientific character."—*Solicitors' Journal.*

"The subject and the work are both very good. The former is well chosen, new, and interesting; the latter has the quality which always distinguishes original research from borrowed labours."—*American Law Review.*

"We are happy to welcome his (Mr. May's) work as an addition to the, we regret to say, brief catalogue of law books conscientiously executed. We can corroborate his own description of his labours that no pains have been spared to make the book as concise and practical as possible, without doing so at the expense of perspicuity, or by the omission of any important points."—*Law Times.*

In one volume, medium 8vo, price 38s., cloth ; or in half-roxburgh, 42s.,

A HISTORY OF THE FORESHORE
AND THE LAW RELATING THERETO.

WITH A HITHERTO UNPUBLISHED TREATISE BY LORD HALE, LORD HALE'S "DE JURE MARIS," AND THE THIRD EDITION OF HALL'S ESSAY ON THE

RIGHTS OF THE CROWN IN THE SEA-SHORE.
WITH NOTES, AND AN APPENDIX RELATING TO FISHERIES.

By STUART A. MOORE, F.S.A.,
OF THE INNER TEMPLE, BARRISTER-AT-LAW.

"This work is nominally a third edition of the late Mr. Hall's essay on the rights of the Crown in the Sea-shore, but in reality is an absolutely new production, for out of some 900 odd pages Hall's essay takes up but 227. Mr. Moore has written a book of great importance, which should mark an epoch in the history of the rights of the Crown and the subject in the *litus maris*, or foreshore of the kingdom. Hall's treatise (with Loveland's notes) is set out with fresh notes by the present editor, who is anything but kindly disposed towards his author, for his notes are nothing but a series of exposures of what he deems to be Hall's errors and misrepresentations. Mr. Moore admits his book to be a brief for the opposite side of the contention supported by Hall, and a more vigorous and argumentative treatise we have scarcely ever seen. Its arguments are clearly and broadly disclosed, and supported by a wealth of facts and cases which show the research of the learned author to have been most full and elaborate. . . . There is no doubt that this is an important work, which must have a considerable influence on that branch of the law with which it deals. That law is contained in ancient and most inaccessible records ; these have now been brought to light, and it may well be that important results to the subject may flow therefrom. The Profession, not to say the general public, owe the learned author a deep debt of gratitude for providing ready to hand such a wealth of materials for founding and building up arguments. Mr. Stuart Moore has written a work which must, unless his contentions are utterly unfounded, at once become the standard text-book on the law of the Sea-shore."—*Law Times*, Dec. 1st.
"Mr. Stuart Moore in his valuable work on the Foreshore."—*The Times*.
"Mr. Stuart Moore's work on the title of the Crown to the land around the coast of England lying between the high and low water mark is something more than an ordinary law book. It is a history, and a very interesting one, of such land and the rights exercised over it from the earliest times to the present day ; and a careful study of the facts contained in these pages can scarcely fail to convince the reader of the inaccuracy of the theory, now so constantly put forward by the Crown, that without the existence of special evidence to the contrary, the land which adjoins riparian property, and which is covered at high tide, belongs to the Crown and not to the owner of the adjoining manor. The list which Mr. Moore gives of places where the question of foreshore has been already raised, and of those as to which evidence on the subject exists amongst the public records, is valuable, though by no means exhaustive ; and the book should certainly find a place in the library of the lord of every riparian manor."—*Morning Post*.

In one volume, 8vo, price 12s., cloth,

A TREATISE ON THE LAW RELATING TO THE

POLLUTION AND OBSTRUCTION OF WATER COURSES ;
TOGETHER WITH A BRIEF SUMMARY OF THE VARIOUS SOURCES OF RIVERS POLLUTION.

By CLEMENT HIGGINS, M.A., F.C.S.,
OF THE INNER TEMPLE, BARRISTER-AT-LAW.

"As a compendium of the law upon a special and rather intricate subject, this treatise cannot but prove of great practical value, and more especially to those who have to advise upon the institution of proceedings under the Rivers Pollution Prevention Act, 1876, or to adjudicate upon those proceedings when brought."—*Irish Law Times*.
"We can recommend Mr. Higgins' Manual as the best guide we possess."—*Public Health*.
"County Court Judges, Sanitary Authorities, and Riparian Owners will find in Mr. Higgins' Treatise a valuable aid in obtaining a clear notion of the Law on the Subject. Mr. Higgins has accomplished a work for which he will readily be recognised as having special fitness on account of his practical acquaintance both with the scientific and the legal aspects of his subject."—*Law Magazine and Review*.
"The volume is very carefully arranged throughout, and will prove of great utility both to miners and to owners of land on the banks of rivers."—*The Mining Journal*.
"Mr. Higgins writes tersely and clearly, while his facts are so well arranged that it is a pleasure to refer to his book for information ; and altogether the work is one which will be found very useful by all interested in the subject to which it relates."—*Engineer*.
"A compact and convenient manual of the law on the subject to which it relates."—*Solicitors' Journal*.

In 8vo, FIFTH EDITION, price 28s., cloth.

MAYNE'S TREATISE
ON
THE LAW OF DAMAGES.

FIFTH EDITION.
REVISED AND PARTLY REWRITTEN.
BY
JOHN D. MAYNE,
OF THE INNER TEMPLE, BARRISTER-AT-LAW;
AND
HIS HONOR JUDGE LUMLEY SMITH, Q.C.

"'Mayne on Damages' has now become almost a classic, and it is one of the books which we cannot afford to have up to date. We are therefore pleased to have a new Edition, and one so well written as that before us. With the authors we regret the increasing size of the volume, but bulk in such a case is better than incompleteness. Every lawyer in practice should have this book, full as it is of practical learning on all branches of the Common Law. The work is unique, and this Edition, like its predecessors, is indispensable."—*Law Journal*, April, 1894.

"Few books have been better kept up to the current law than this treatise. The earlier part of the book was remodelled in the last edition, and in the present edition the chapter on Penalties and Liquidated Damages has been rewritten, no doubt in consequence of, or with regard to, the elaborate and exhaustive judgment of the late Master of the Rolls in *Wallis* v. *Smith* (31 W. R. 214; L. R. 21 Ch. D. 243). The treatment of the subject by the authors is admirably clear and concise. Upon the point involved in *Wallis* v. *Smith* they say : 'The result is that an agreement with various covenants of different importance is not to be governed by any inflexible rule peculiar to itself, but is to be dealt with as coming under the general rule, that the intention of the parties themselves is to be considered. If they have said that in the case of any breach a fixed sum is to be paid, then they will be kept to their agreement, unless it would lead to such an absurdity or injustice that it must be assumed that they did not mean what they said.' This is a very fair summary of the judgments in *Wallis* v. *Smith*, especially of that of Lord Justice Cotton ; and it supplies the nearest approach which can be given at present to a rule for practical guidance. We can heartily commend this as a carefully edited edition of a thoroughly good book."—*Solicitors' Journal*.

"*During the twenty-two years which have elapsed since the publication of this well-known work, its reputation has been steadily growing, and it has long since become the recognised authority on the important subject of which it treats.*"—LAW MAGAZINE AND REVIEW.

"This edition of what has become a standard work has the advantage of appearing under the supervision of the original author as well as of Mr. Lumley Smith, the editor of the second edition. The result is most satisfactory. Mr. Lumley Smith's edition was ably and conscientiously prepared, and we are glad to find that the reader still enjoys the benefit of his accuracy and learning. At the same time the book has doubtless been improved by the reappearance of its author as co-editor. The earlier part, indeed, has been to a considerable extent entirely rewritten.

"Mr. Mayne's remarks on damages in actions of tort are brief. We agree with him that in such actions the courts are governed by far looser principles than in contracts ; indeed, sometimes it is impossible to say they are governed by any principles at all. In actions for injuries to the person or reputation, for example, a judge cannot do more than give a general direction to the jury to give what the facts proved in their judgment required. And, according to the better opinion, they may give damages 'for example's sake,' and mulct a rich man more heavily than a poor one. In actions for injuries to property, however, 'vindictive' or 'exemplary' damages cannot, except in very rare cases, be awarded, but must be limited, as in contract, to the actual harm sustained.

"It is needless to comment upon the arrangement of the subjects in this edition, in which no alteration has been made. The editors modestly express a hope that all the English as well as the principal Irish decisions up to the date have been included, and we believe from our own examination that the hope is well founded. We may regret that, warned by the growing bulk of the book, the editors have not included any fresh American cases, but we feel that the omission was unavoidable. We should add that the whole work has been thoroughly revised."—*Solicitors' Journal*.

"*This text-book is so well known, not only as the highest authority on the subject treated of but as one of the best text-books ever written, that it would be idle for us to speak of it in the words of commendation that it deserves. It is work that no practising lawyer can do without.*"—CANADA LAW JOURNAL.

32   STEVENS & HAYNES, BELL YARD, TEMPLE BAR.

In crown 8vo, price 4s. 6d., cloth,

ABSTRACT DRAWING. Containing Instructions on
the Drawing of Abstracts of Title, and an Illustrative Appendix. By C. E. SCOTT, Solicitor.

"This little book is intended for the assistance of those who have the framing of abstracts of title entrusted to their care. It contains a number of useful rules, and an illustrative appendix."—*Law Times.*
"A handy book for all articled clerks."—*Law Students' Journal.*
"Solicitors who have articled clerks would save themselves much trouble if they furnished their clerks with a copy of this little book before putting them on to draft an abstract of a heap of title deeds."—*Law Notes.*
"The book ought to be perused by all law students and articled clerks."—*Red Tape.*

Second Edition, in crown 8vo, price 7s., cloth,

THE LAW RELATING TO CLUBS.
BY THE LATE JOHN WERTHEIMER, BARRISTER-AT-LAW.
Second Edition, by A. W. CHASTER, Barrister-at-Law.

"A convenient handbook, drawn up with great judgment and perspicuity."—*Morning Post.*
"Both useful and interesting to those interested in club management."—*Law Times.*
"Mr. Wertheimer's history of the cases is complete and well arranged."—*Saturday Review.*

"This is a very neat little book on an interesting subject. The law is accurately and well expressed."—*Law Journal.*
"This is a very handy and complete little work. This excellent little treatise should lie on the table of every club."—*Pump Court.*

In 8vo, price 2s., sewed,

TABLE of the FOREIGN MERCANTILE LAWS and CODES
in Force in the Principal States of EUROPE and AMERICA. By CHARLES LYON-CAEN, Professeur agrégé à la Faculté de Droit de Paris; Professeur à l'Ecole libre des Sciences politiques. Translated by NAPOLEON ARGLES, Solicitor, Paris.

In 8vo, price 1s., sewed,

A GUIDE TO THE FRENCH LAWS OF 1889, ON NATION-
ALITY AND MILITARY SERVICE, as affecting British Subjects. By A. PAVITT, Solicitor, Paris.

In one volume, demy 8vo, price 10s. 6d., cloth,

PRINCIPLES OF THE LAW OF STOPPAGE IN TRANSITU,
RETENTION, and DELIVERY. By JOHN HOUSTON, of the Middle Temple, Barrister-at-Law.

In 8vo, price 10s., cloth,

THE TRIAL OF ADELAIDE BARTLETT FOR
MURDER; Complete and Revised Report. Edited by EDWARD BEAL, B.A., of the Middle Temple, Barrister-at-Law. With a Preface by EDWARD CLARKE, Q.C., M.P.

In 8vo, price 10s. 6d., cloth,
A REPORT OF THE CASE OF

THE QUEEN v. GURNEY AND OTHERS,
In the Court of Queen's Bench before the Lord Chief Justice COCKBURN. With Introduction, containing History of the Case, and Examination of the Cases at Law and Equity applicable to it. By W. F. FINLASON, Barrister-at-Law.

In royal 8vo, price 10s. 6d., cloth,

THE PRACTICE OF EQUITY BY WAY OF REVIVOR AND SUPPLEMENT.
With Forms of Orders and Appendix of Bills. By LOFTUS LEIGH PEMBERTON, of the Chancery Registrar's Office.

In 8vo, price 12s. 6d., cloth,

THE ANNUAL DIGEST OF MERCANTILE CASES FOR THE YEARS 1885 AND 1886.

BEING A DIGEST OF THE DECISIONS OF THE ENGLISH, SCOTCH AND IRISH COURTS ON MATTERS RELATING TO COMMERCE.

By JAMES A. DUNCAN, M.A., LL.B., Trin. Coll., Camb.,
AND OF THE INNER TEMPLE, BARRISTER-AT-LAW.

In 8vo, 1878, price 6s., cloth,

THE

LAW RELATING TO CHARITIES,

ESPECIALLY WITH REFERENCE TO THE VALIDITY AND CONSTRUCTION OF

CHARITABLE BEQUESTS AND CONVEYANCES.

By FERDINAND M. WHITEFORD, of Lincoln's Inn, Barrister-at-Law.

Vols. I., II., III., IV., and V., Part I., price 5l. 7s.

REPORTS OF THE DECISIONS OF THE

JUDGES FOR THE TRIAL OF ELECTION PETITIONS

IN ENGLAND AND IRELAND.

PURSUANT TO THE PARLIAMENTARY ELECTIONS ACT, 1868.

By EDWARD LOUGHLIN O'MALLEY AND HENRY HARDCASTLE.

₊* *Vol. IV. Part III. and all after are Edited by* J. S. SANDARS *and* A. P. P. KEEP, *Barristers-at-Law.*

In 8vo, price 12s., cloth,

THE LAW OF FIXTURES, in the principal relation of Landlord and Tenant, and in all other or general relations. Fourth Edition. By ARCHIBALD BROWN, M.A. Edin. and Oxon., and B.C.L. Oxon., of the Middle Temple, Barrister-at-Law.

In one volume, 8vo, price 28s., cloth,

THE LAW RELATING TO PUBLIC WORSHIP;

With special reference to Matters of Ritual and Ornamentation, and the Means of Securing the Due Observance thereof, and containing in extenso, with Notes and References, The Public Worship Regulation Act, 1874; The Church Discipline Act; the various Acts of Uniformity; the Liturgies of 1549, 1552, and 1559, compared with the Present Rubric; the Canons; the Articles; and the Injunctions, Advertisements, and other Original Documents of Legal Authority. By SEWARD BRICE, LL.D., of the Inner Temple, Barrister-at-Law.

Stevens and Haynes' Series of Reprints of the Early Reporters.

SIR BARTHOLOMEW SHOWER'S PARLIAMENTARY CASES.

In 8vo, 1876, price 4*l.* 4*s.*, best calf binding,

SHOWER'S CASES IN PARLIAMENT
RESOLVED AND ADJUDGED UPON PETITIONS & WRITS OF ERROR.
FOURTH EDITION.
CONTAINING ADDITIONAL CASES NOT HITHERTO REPORTED.
REVISED AND EDITED BY
RICHARD LOVELAND LOVELAND,
OF THE INNER TEMPLE, BARRISTER-AT-LAW; EDITOR OF "KELYNG'S CROWN CASES," AND "HALL'S ESSAY ON THE RIGHTS OF THE CROWN IN THE SEASHORE."

"Messrs. STEVENS & HAYNES, the successful publishers of the Reprints of Bellewe, Cooke, Cunningham, Brookes's New Cases, Choyce Cases in Chancery, William Kelynge and Kelyng's Crown Cases, determined to issue a new or fourth Edition of Shower's Cases in Parliament.

"The volume, although beautifully printed on old-fashioned Paper, in old-fashioned type, instead of being in the quarto is in the more convenient octavo form, and contains several additional cases not to be found in any of the previous editions of the work.

"These are all cases of importance, worthy of being ushered into the light of the world by enterprising publishers.

"Shower's Cases are models for reporters, even in our day. The statements of the case, the arguments of counsel, and the opinions of the Judges, are all clearly and ably given.

"This new edition with an old face of these valuable reports, under the able editorship of R. L. Loveland, Esq., should, in the language of the advertisement, 'be welcomed by the profession, as well as enable the custodians of public libraries to complete or add to their series of English Law Reports.'"—*Canada Law Journal.*

BELLEWE'S CASES, T. RICHARD II.

In 8vo, 1869, price 3*l.* 3*s.*, bound in calf antique,

LES ANS DU ROY RICHARD LE SECOND.
Collect' ensembl' hors les abridgments de Statham, Fitzherbert et Brooke. Per RICHARD BELLEWE, de Lincolns Inne. 1585. Reprinted from the Original Edition.

"No public library in the world, where English law finds a place, should be without a copy of this edition of Bellewe."—*Canada Law Journal.*

"We have here a *fac-simile* edition of Bellewe, and it is really the most beautiful and admirable reprint that has appeared at any time. It is a perfect gem of antique printing, and forms a most interesting monument of our early legal history. It belongs to the same class of works as the Year Book of Edward I. and other similar works which have been printed in our own time under the auspices of the Master of the Rolls; but is far superior to any of them, and is in this respect highly creditable to the spirit and enterprise of private publishers. The work is an important link in our legal history; there are no year books of the reign of Richard II., and Bellewe supplied the only substitute by carefully extracting and collecting all the cases he could find, and he did it in the most convenient form—that of alphabetical arrangement in the order of subjects, so that the work is a digest as well as a book of law reports. It is in fact a collection of cases of the reign of Richard II., arranged according to their subjects in alphabetical order. It is therefore one of the most intelligible and interesting legal memorials of the Middle Ages."—*Law Times.*

CUNNINGHAM'S REPORTS.
In 8vo, 1871, price 3*l.* 3*s.*, calf antique,

CUNNINGHAM'S (T.) Reports in K. B., 7 to 10 Geo. II.; to which is prefixed a Proposal for rendering the Laws of England clear and certain, humbly offered to the Consideration of both Houses of Parliament. Third edition, with numerous Corrections. By THOMAS TOWNSEND BUCKNILL, Barrister-at-Law.

"The instructive chapter which precedes the cases, entitled 'A proposal for rendering the Laws of England clear and certain,' gives the value of many of the reported cases. That chapter begins with words which ought, for the information of every people, to be printed in letters of gold. They are as follows: 'Nothing conduces more to the peace and prosperity of every nation than good laws and the due execution of them.' The history of the civil law is then rapidly traced. Next a history is given of English Reporters, beginning with the reporters of the Year Books from 1 Edw. III. to 12 Hen. VIII.—being near 200 years—and afterwards to the time of the author."—*Canada Law Journal.*

Stevens and Haynes' Series of Reprints of the Early Reporters.

CHOYCE CASES IN CHANCERY.

In 8vo, 1870, price 2*l.* 2*s.*, calf antique,

THE PRACTICE OF THE HIGH COURT OF CHANCERY.

With the Nature of the several Offices belonging to that Court. And the Reports of many Cases wherein Relief hath been there had, and where denyed.

"This volume, in paper, type, and binding (like 'Bellewe's Cases') is a fac-simile of the antique edition All who buy the one should buy the other."—*Canada Law Journal.*

In 8vo, 1872, price 3*l.* 3*s.*, calf antique,

SIR G. COOKE'S COMMON PLEAS REPORTS
IN THE REIGNS OF QUEEN ANNE, AND KINGS GEORGE I. AND II.

The Third Edition, with Additional Cases and References contained in the Notes taken from L. C. J. EYRE'S MSS. by Mr. Justice NARES, edited by THOMAS TOWNSEND BUCKNILL, of the Inner Temple, Barrister-at-Law.

"Law books never can die or remain long dead so long as Stevens and Haynes are willing to continue them or revive them when dead. It is certainly surprising to see with what facial accuracy an old volume of Reports may be produced by these modern publishers, whose good taste is only equalled by their enterprise."—*Canada Law Journal.*

BROOKE'S NEW CASES WITH MARCH'S TRANSLATION.

In 8vo, 1873, price 4*l.* 4*s.*, calf antique,

BROOKE'S (Sir Robert) New Cases in the time of Henry VIII., Edward VI., and Queen Mary, collected out of BROOKE'S Abridgement, and arranged under years, with a table, together with MARCH'S (John) *Translation of* BROOKE'S New Cases in the time of Henry VIII., Edward VI., and Queen Mary, collected out of BROOKE'S Abridgement, and reduced alphabetically under their proper heads and titles, with a table of the principal matters. In one handsome volume. 8vo. 1873.

"Both the original and the translation having long been very scarce, and the mispaging and other errors in March's translation making a new and corrected edition peculiarly desirable, Messrs. Stevens and Haynes have reprinted the two books in one volume uniform with the preceding volumes of the series of Early Reports."—*Canada Law Journal.*

KELYNGE'S (W.) REPORTS.

In 8vo, 1873, price 4*l.* 4*s.*, calf antique,

KELYNGE'S (William) Reports of Cases in Chancery, the King's Bench, &c., from the 3rd to the 9th year of his late Majesty King George II., during which time Lord King was Chancellor, and the Lords Raymond and Hardwicke were Chief Justices of England. To which are added, seventy New Cases not in the First Edition. Third Edition. In one handsome volume. 8vo. 1873.

KELYNG'S (SIR JOHN) CROWN CASES.

In 8vo, 1873, price 4*l.* 4*s.*, calf antique,

KELYNG'S (Sir J.) Reports of Divers Cases in Pleas of the Crown in the Reign of King Charles II., with Directions to Justices of the Peace, and others; to which are added, Three Modern Cases, viz., Armstrong and Lisle, the King and Plummer, the Queen and Mawgridge. Third Edition, *containing several additional Cases never before printed,* together with a TREATISE UPON THE LAW AND PROCEEDINGS IN CASES OF HIGH TREASON, first published in 1793. The whole carefully revised and edited by RICHARD LOVELAND LOVELAND, of the Inner Temple, Barrister-at-Law.

"We look upon this volume as one of the most important and valuable of the unique reprints of Messrs. Stevens and Haynes. Little do we know of the mines of legal wealth that lie buried in the old law books. But a careful examination, either of the reports or of the treatise embodied in the volume now before us, will give the reader some idea of the goodservice rendered by Messrs. Stevens and Haynes to the profession. . . . Should occasion arise, the Crown prosecutor, as well as counsel for the prisoner, will find in this volume a complete *vade mecum* of the law of high treason and proceedings in relation thereto."—*Canada Law Journal.*

Second Edition, in 8vo, price 26s., cloth,

A CONCISE TREATISE ON
PRIVATE INTERNATIONAL JURISPRUDENCE,
BASED ON THE DECISIONS IN THE ENGLISH COURTS.

By JOHN ALDERSON FOOTE,

OF LINCOLN'S INN, BARRISTER-AT-LAW ; CHANCELLOR'S LEGAL MEDALLIST AND SENIOR WHEWELL SCHOLAR OF INTERNATIONAL LAW, CAMBRIDGE UNIVERSITY, 1873 ; SENIOR STUDENT IN JURISPRUDENCE AND ROMAN LAW, INNS OF COURT EXAMINATION, HILARY TERM, 1874.

"This work seems to us likely to prove of considerable use to all English lawyers who have to deal with questions of private international law. Since the publication of Mr. Westlake's valuable treatise, twenty years ago, the judicial decisions of English courts bearing upon different parts of this subject have greatly increased in number, and it is full time that these decisions should be examined, and that the conclusions to be deduced from them should be systematically set forth in a treatise. Moreover, Mr. Foote has done this well."—*Solicitors' Journal.*

"Mr. Foote has done his work very well, and the book will be useful to all who have to deal with the class of cases in which English law alone is not sufficient to settle the question."—*Saturday Review,* March 8, 1879.

"The author's object has been to reduce into order the mass of materials already accumulated in the shape of explanation and actual decision on the interesting matter of which he treats ; and to construct a framework of private international law, not from the *dicta* of jurists so much as from judicial decisions in English Courts which have superseded them. And it is here, in compiling and arranging in a concise form this valuable material, that Mr. Foote's wide range of knowledge and legal acumen bear such good fruit. As a guide and assistant to the student of international law, the whole treatise will be invaluable ; while a table of cases and a general index will enable him to find what he wants without trouble."—*Standard.*

"The recent decisions on points of international law (and there have been a large number since Westlake's publication) have been well stated. So far as we have observed, no case of any importance has been omitted, and the leading cases have been fully analysed. The author does not hesitate to criticise the grounds of a decision when these appear to him to conflict with the proper rule of law. Most of his criticisms seem to us very just. . . . . On the whole, we can recommend Mr. Foote's treatise as a useful addition to our text-books, and we expect it will rapidly find its way into the hands of practising lawyers."
—*The Journal of Jurisprudence and Scottish Law Magazine.*

"Mr. Foote has evidently borne closely in mind the needs of Students of Jurisprudence as well as those of the Practitioners. For both, the fact that his work is almost entirely one of Case-law will commend it as one useful alike in Chambers and in Court."—*Law Magazine and Review.*

"Mr. Foote's book will be useful to the student. . . . . . One of the best points of Mr. Foote's book is the 'Continuous Summary,' which occupies about thirty pages, and is divided into four parts—Persons, Property, Acts, and Procedure. Mr. Foote remarks that these summaries are not in any way intended as an attempt at codification. However that may be, they are a digest which reflects high credit on the author's assiduity and capacity. They are 'meant merely to guide the student ;' but they will do much more than guide him. They will enable him to get such a grasp of the subject as will render the reading of the text easy and fruitful."—*Law Journal.*

"This book is well adapted to be used both as a text-book for students and a book of reference for practising barristers."—*Bar Examination Journal.*

"This is a book which supplies the want which has long been felt for a really good modern treatise on Private International Law adapted to the every-day requirements of the English Practitioner. The whole volume, although designed for the use of the practitioner, is so moderate in size—an octavo of 500 pages only—and the arrangement and development of the subject so well conceived and executed, that it will amply repay perusal by those whose immediate object may be not the actual decisions of a knotty point but the satisfactory disposal of an examination paper."—*Oxford and Cambridge Undergraduates' Journal.*

"Since the publication, some twenty years ago, of Mr. Westlake's Treatise, Mr. Foote's book is, in our opinion, the best work on private international law which has appeared in the English language. . . . . The work is executed with much ability, and will doubtless be found of great value by all persons who have to consider questions on private international law."—*Athenæum.*

STEVENS & HAYNES, BELL YARD, TEMPLE BAR.

THE
Law Magazine and Review,
AND
QUARTERLY DIGEST OF ALL REPORTED CASES.
Price FIVE SHILLINGS each Number.

No. CCXVIII. (Vol. I, No. I. of the New QUARTERLY Series.) November, 1875.
No. CCXIX. (Vol. I, 4th Series No. II.) February, 1876.
N.B.—These two Numbers are out of print.

No. CCXX.   (Vol. 1, 4th Series No. III.)   For May, 1876.
No. CCXXI.   (Vol. 1, 4th Series No. IV.)   For August, 1876.

Nos. CCXXII. to CCXLIX. (Vol. 2, 4th Series, to Vol. 8, 4th Series, Nos. V. to XXXII.)
November, 1876, to August, 1883.

Nos. CCL. to CCLIII. (Vol. 9, 4th Series, Nos. XXXIII. to XXXVI.),
November, 1883, to August, 1884.

Nos. CCLIV. to CCLVII. (Vol. 9, 4th Series, Nos. XXXVII. to XL.),
November, 1884, to August, 1885.

Nos. CCLVIII. to CCLXI. (Vol. X., 4th Series, Nos. XLI. to XLIV.),
November, 1885, to August, 1886.

Nos. CCLXII. to CCLXV. (Vol. XI., 4th Series, Nos. XLV. to XLVIII.),
November, 1886, to August, 1887.

Nos. CCLXVI. to CCLXIX. (Vol. XII., 4th Series, Nos. XLIX. to LII.),
November, 1887, to August, 1888.

Nos. CCLXX. to CCLXXIII. (Vol. XIII., 4th Series, Nos. LIII. to LVI.),
November, 1888, to August, 1889.

Nos. CCLXXIV. to CCLXXVII. (Vol. XIV., 4th Series, Nos. LVII. to LX.),
November, 1889, to August, 1890.

Nos. CCLXXVIII. to CCLXXXI. (Vol. XV., 4th Series, Nos. LXI. to LXIV.),
November, 1890, to August, 1891.

Nos. CCLXXXII. to CCLXXXV. (Vol. XVI., 4th Series, Nos. LXV. to LXVIII.),
November, 1891, to August, 1892.

Nos. CCLXXXVI. to CCLXXXIX. (Vol. XVII., 4th Series, Nos. LXIX. to LXXII.)
November, 1892, to August, 1893.

Nos. CCXC. to CCXCIII. (Vol. XVIII., 4th Series, Nos. LXXIII. to LXXVI.),
November, 1893, to August, 1894.

Nos. CCXCIV. to CCXCVII. (Vol. XIX., 4th Series, Nos. LXXVII. to LXXX.),
November, 1894, to August, 1895.

Nos. CCXCVIII. to CCCV. (Vols. XX. & XXI., 4th Series, Nos. LXXXI. to LXXXVIII.),
November, 1895, to August, 1897.

An Annual Subscription of 20s., paid in advance to the Publishers, will secure the receipt of the LAW MAGAZINE, free by post, within the United Kingdom, or for 24s. to the Colonies and Abroad.

Fifth Edition, revised and enlarged, 8vo, price 32s. net.

A TREATISE ON HINDU LAW AND USAGE.

By JOHN D. MAYNE, of the Inner Temple, Barrister-at-Law, Author of "A Treatise on Damages," &c.

"A new work from the pen of so established an authority as Mr. Mayne cannot fail to be welcome to the legal profession. In his present volume the late Officiating Advocate-General at Madras has drawn upon the stores of his long experience in Southern India, and has produced a work of value alike to the practitioner at the Indian Bar, or at home, in appeal cases, and to the scientific jurist.

"To all who, whether as practitioners or administrators, or as students of the science of jurisprudence, desire a thoughtful and suggestive work of reference on Hindu Law and Usage, we heartily recommend the careful perusal of Mr. Mayne's valuable treatise."—*Law Magazine and Review.*

In 8vo, 1877, price 15s., cloth,

A DIGEST OF HINDU LAW,

AS ADMINISTERED IN THE COURTS OF THE MADRAS PRESIDENCY.
ARRANGED AND ANNOTATED
By H. S. CUNNINGHAM, M.A., Advocate-General, Madras.

DUTCH LAW.

In 1 Vol., 8vo, price 40s., cloth,

THE OPINIONS OF GROTIUS, As contained in the Hollandsche Consultatien en Advijsen. Collated, translated, and annotated by D. P. DE BRUYN, B.A., LL.B., Ebden Essayist of the University of the Cape of Good Hope ; Advocate of the Supreme Court of the Colony of the Cape of Good Hope, and of the High Court of the South African Republic. With Facsimile Portrait of Mr. HUGO DE GROOT.

In 2 Vols., Royal 8vo, price 90s., cloth,

VAN LEEUWEN'S COMMENTARIES ON THE ROMAN-DUTCH LAW. Revised and Edited with Notes in Two Volumes by C. W. DECKER, Advocate. Translated from the original Dutch by J. G. KOTZÉ, LL.B., of the Inner Temple, Barrister-at-Law, and Chief Justice of the Transvaal. With Facsimile Portrait in the Edition by DECKER of 1780.

⁎ Vol. II. can be had separately, price 50s.

In 8vo, price 15s. 6d., net.

VOET'S TITLES ON VINDICATIONES AND INTERDICTA, Or the Roman Dutch Law of Actions to Assert Rights of Property, including Injunctions and Possessory Actions, translated into English with side-notes; viz., Book VI. Titles I. to III., Book VII. Title VI., Book VIII. Title V., Book XX. Title IV., and Book XLIII. Titles I., XVI. to XXXIII., of Voet's Commentary on the Pandects, with a Scientific and General Introduction, Notes Explanatory of the Roman Civil and Roman Dutch, and English Law, Notes of Ceylon Enactments and Practice, and Decisions of the Supreme Court, Ceylon, etc. By JOHN J. CASIE CHITTY, Barrister-at-Law, Advocate, High Court, Madras, and Supreme Court, Ceylon.

In 8vo, price 42s., cloth,

THE JUDICIAL PRACTICE OF THE COLONY OF THE CAPE OF GOOD HOPE AND OF SOUTH AFRICA GENERALLY. With suitable and copious Practical Forms, subjoined to, and illustrating the Practice of the several Subjects treated of. By C. H. VAN ZYL, Attorney-at-Law, Notary Public, and Conveyancer, etc. etc.

In Crown 8vo, price 31s. 6d., boards,

THE INTRODUCTION TO DUTCH JURISPRUDENCE OF HUGO GROTIUS, with Notes by Simon van Groenwegen van der Made, and References to Van der Keessel's Theses and Schorer's Notes. Translated by A. F. S. MAASDORP, B.A., of the Inner Temple, Barrister-at-Law.

In 12mo, price 15s. net, boards,

SELECT THESES ON THE LAWS OF HOLLAND & ZEELAND. Being a Commentary of Hugo Grotius' Introduction to Dutch Jurisprudence, and intended to supply certain defects therein, and to determine some of the more celebrated Controversies on the Law of Holland. By D. G. VAN DER KESSEL, Advocate. Translated by C. A. LORENZ, Barrister-at-Law. Second Edition. With a Biographical Notice of the Author by Professor J. DE WAL, of Leyden.

THE
Bar Examination Annual
FOR 1894.
(In Continuation of the Bar Examination Journal.)

Price 3s.

EXAMINATION PAPERS, 1893.
FOR PASS, HONORS, AND BARSTOW SCHOLARSHIP.
RESULT OF EXAMINATIONS.
NAMES OF SUCCESSFUL CANDIDATES.
EXAMINATION REGULATIONS FOR 1894.
A GUIDE TO THE BAR.
LEADING DECISIONS AND STATUTES OF 1894.
NEW BOOKS AND NEW EDITIONS.

W. D. EDWARDS, LL.B.,
OF LINCOLN'S INN, BARRISTER-AT-LAW.

In 8vo, price 18s. each, cloth,

THE BAR EXAMINATION JOURNAL, VOLS. IV., V.,

VI., VII., VIII., IX. & X. Containing the Examination Questions and Answers from Easter Term, 1878, to Hilary Term, 1892, with List of Successful Candidates at each examination, Notes on the Law of Property, and a Synopsis of Recent Legislation of importance to Students, and other information.

BY A. D. TYSSEN AND W. D. EDWARDS, Barristers-at-Law.

In 8vo, price 8s., cloth,

SHORT PRACTICAL COMPANY FORMS.

By T. EUSTACE SMITH, of the Inner Temple and Lincoln's Inn, Barrister-at-Law, Author of "A Summary of the Law of Companies," etc., assisted by ROLAND E. VAUGHAN WILLIAMS, of the Inner Temple, Barrister-at-Law.

REVIEW.

"This collection of Company Forms should certainly prove of service to secretaries, directors, and others interested, in the practical working of companies. . . . The forms themselves are short and to the point."—*Law Times.*

Sixth Edition. In 8vo, price 9s. cloth,

A SUMMARY OF JOINT STOCK COMPANIES' LAW.

BY T. EUSTACE SMITH,
OF THE INNER TEMPLE, BARRISTER-AT-LAW.

"The author of this handbook tells us that, when an articled student reading for the final examination, he felt the want of such a work as that before us, wherein could be found the main principles of law relating to joint-stock companies . . . Law students may well read it; for Mr. Smith has very wisely been at the pains of giving his authority for all his statements of the law or of practice, as applied to joint-stock company business usually transacted in solicitors' chambers. In fact, Mr. Smith has by his little book offered a fresh inducement to students to make themselves—at all events, to some extent—acquainted with company law as a separate branch of study."—*Law Times.*

"These pages give, in the words of the Preface, 'as briefly and concisely as possible a general view both of the principles and practice of the law affecting companies.' The work is excellently printed, and authorities are cited; but in no case is the very language of the statutes copied. The plan is good, and shows both grasp and neatness, and, both amongst students and laymen, Mr. Smith's book ought to meet a ready sale."—*Law Journal.*

"The book is one from which we have derived a large amount of valuable information, and we can heartily and conscientiously recommend it to our readers."—*Oxford and Cambridge Undergraduates' Journal.*

In 8vo, Sixth Edition, price 9s., cloth,

THE MARRIED WOMEN'S PROPERTY ACTS;
1870, 1874, 1882 and 1884,
WITH COPIOUS AND EXPLANATORY NOTES, AND AN APPENDIX OF THE ACTS RELATING TO MARRIED WOMEN.

By ARCHIBALD BROWN, M.A., Edinburgh and Oxon., and the Middle Temple, Barrister-at-Law. Being the Sixth Edition of The Married Women's Property Acts. By the late J. R. GRIFFITHS, B.A. Oxon., of Lincoln's Inn, Barrister-at-Law.

"Upon the whole, we are of opinion that this is the best work upon the subject which has been issued since the passing of the recent Act. Its position as a well-established manual of acknowledged worth gives it at starting a considerable advantage over new books; and this advantage has been well maintained by the intelligent treatment of the Editor."—*Solicitors' Journal.*

"The notes are full, but anything rather than tedious reading, and the law contained in them is good, and verified by reported cases. . . . A distinct feature of the work is its copious index, practically a summary of the marginal headings of the various paragraphs in the body of the text. This book is worthy of all success."—*Law Magazine.*

In 8vo, price 12s., cloth,

THE LAW OF NEGLIGENCE.
SECOND EDITION.

By ROBERT CAMPBELL, of Lincoln's Inn, Barrister-at-Law, and Advocate of the Scotch Bar.

"No less an authority than the late Mr. Justice Willes, in his judgment in *Oppenheim* v. *White Lion Hotel Co.*, characterised Mr. Campbell's 'Law of Negligence' as a 'very good book;' and since very good books are by no means plentiful, when compared with the numbers of indifferent ones which annually issue from the press, we think the profession will be thankful to the author of this new edition brought down to date. It is indeed an able and scholarly treatise on a somewhat difficult branch of law, in the treatment of which the author's knowledge of Roman and Scotch Jurisprudence has stood him in good stead. We confidently recommend it alike to the student and the practitioner."—*Law Magazine.*

In 8vo, price 10s. 6d. net.

THE LAW AND PRIVILEGES RELATING TO THE ATTORNEY-GENERAL AND SOLICITOR-GENERAL OF ENGLAND,
with a History from the Earliest Periods, and a Series of King's Attorneys and Attorneys and Solicitors-General from the reign of Henry III. to the 60th of Victoria. By J. W. NORTON-KYSHE, of Lincoln's Inn, Barrister-at-Law.

BIBLIOTHECA LEGUM.

In 12mo (nearly 400 pages), price 2s., cloth,

A CATALOGUE OF LAW BOOKS.
Including all the Reports in the various Courts of England, Scotland, and Ireland; with a Supplement to December, 1884. By HENRY G. STEVENS and ROBERT W. HAYNES, Law Publishers.

In small 4to, price 2s., cloth, beautifully printed, with a large margin, for the special use of Librarians,

A CATALOGUE OF THE REPORTS IN THE VARIOUS COURTS OF THE UNITED KINGDOM OF GREAT BRITAIN AND IRELAND.
ARRANGED BOTH IN ALPHABETICAL & CHRONOLOGICAL ORDER. By STEVENS & HAYNES, Law Publishers.

Second Edition, much enlarged, in 8vo, price 20s., cloth,

CHAPTERS ON THE
LAW RELATING TO THE COLONIES.

To which are appended TOPICAL INDEXES of CASES DECIDED in the PRIVY COUNCIL on Appeal from the Colonies, Channel Islands and the Isle of Man, and of Cases relating to the Colonies decided in the English Courts otherwise than on Appeal from the Colonies.

BY CHARLES JAMES TARRING, M.A.,

ASSISTANT JUDGE OF H.B.M. SUPREME CONSULAR COURT, CONSTANTINOPLE, AND H.M.'S CONSUL; AUTHOR OF "BRITISH CONSULAR JURISDICTION IN THE EAST," "A TURKISH GRAMMAR," ETC.

CONTENTS.

Table of Cases Cited.
Table of Statutes Cited.

Introductory.—Definition of a Colony.
Chapter I.—The laws to which the Colonies are subject.
Section 1.—In newly-discovered countries.
Section 2.—In conquered or ceded countries.
Section 3.—Generally.
Chapter II.—The Executive.
Section 1.—The Governor.
  A.—Nature of his office, power, and duties.
  B.—Liability to answer for his acts.
    I.—Civilly.
      , 1. a.—In the courts of his Government.
      b.—In the English courts.
      2.—For what causes of action.
    II.—Criminally.
Section 2.—The Executive Council.
Chapter III.—The Legislative Power.
Section 1.—Classification of colonies.
Section 2.—Colonies with responsible government.
Section 3.—Privileges and powers of colonial Legislative Assemblies.

Chapter IV.—The Judiciary and the Bar.
Chapter V.—Appeals from the Colonies.
Chapter VI.—Imperial Statutes relating to the Colonies.
Section 1.—Imperial Statutes relating to the Colonies in general.
Section 2.—Subjects of Imperial Legislation relating to the Colonies in general.
Section 3.—Imperial Statutes relating to particular Colonies.

Topical Index of Cases decided in the Privy Council on appeal from the Colonies, the Channel Islands, and the Isle of Man.
Index of some Topics of English Law dealt with in the Cases.
Topical Index of Cases relating to the Colonies decided in the English Courts otherwise than on appeal from the Colonies.
Index of Names of Cases.

Appendix I.
  "   II.

GENERAL INDEX.

In 8vo, price 10s., cloth,

THE TAXATION OF COSTS IN THE CROWN OFFICE.

COMPRISING A COLLECTION OF

BILLS OF COSTS IN THE VARIOUS MATTERS TAXABLE IN THAT OFFICE;

INCLUDING

COSTS UPON THE PROSECUTION OF FRAUDULENT BANKRUPTS, AND ON APPEALS FROM INFERIOR COURTS;

TOGETHER WITH

A TABLE OF COURT FEES,

AND A SCALE OF COSTS USUALLY ALLOWED TO SOLICITORS, ON THE TAXATION OF COSTS ON THE CROWN SIDE OF THE QUEEN'S BENCH DIVISION OF THE HIGH COURT OF JUSTICE.

BY FREDK. H. SHORT,

CHIEF CLERK IN THE CROWN OFFICE.

"This is decidedly a useful work on the subject of those costs which are liable to be taxed before the Queen's Coroner and Attorney (for which latter name that of 'Solicitor' might now well be substituted), or before the master of the Crown Office; in fact, such a book is almost indispensable when preparing costs for taxation in the Crown Office, or when taxing an opponent's costs. Country solicitors will find the scale relating to bankruptcy prosecutions of especial use, as such costs are taxed in the Crown Office. The 'general observations' constitute a useful feature in this manual."—*Law Times.*

"The recent revision of the old scale of costs in the Crown Office renders the appearance of this work particularly opportune, and it cannot fail to be welcomed by practitioners. Mr. Short gives, in the first place, a scale of costs usually allowed to solicitors on the taxation of costs in the Crown Office, and then bills of costs in various matters. These are well arranged and clearly printed."—*Solicitors' Journal.*

Just Published, in 8vo, price 7s. 6d., cloth,
BRITISH CONSULAR JURISDICTION IN THE EAST,
WITH TOPICAL INDICES OF CASES ON APPEAL FROM, AND RELATING TO, CONSULAR COURTS AND CONSULS;
Also a Collection of Statutes concerning Consuls.

By C. J. TARRING, M.A.,
ASSISTANT-JUDGE OF H.B.M. SUPREME CONSULAR COURT FOR THE LEVANT.

In one volume, 8vo, price 8s. 6d., cloth,
A COMPLETE TREATISE UPON THE
NEW LAW OF PATENTS, DESIGNS, & TRADE MARKS,
CONSISTING OF THE PATENTS, DESIGNS, AND TRADE MARKS ACT, 1883, WITH THE RULES AND FORMS, FULLY ANNOTATED WITH CASES, &c.
And a Statement of the Principles of the Law upon those subjects, with a Time Table and Copious Index.

By EDWARD MORTON DANIEL,
OF LINCOLN'S INN, BARRISTER-AT-LAW, ASSOCIATE OF THE INSTITUTE OF PATENT AGENTS.

In 8vo, price 8s., cloth,
The TRADE MARKS REGISTRATION ACT, 1875,
And the Rules thereunder; THE MERCHANDISE MARKS ACT, 1862, with an Introduction containing a SUMMARY OF THE LAW OF TRADE MARKS, together with practical Notes and Instructions, and a copious INDEX. By EDWARD MORTON DANIEL, of Lincoln's Inn, Barrister-at-Law.

Second Edition, in one volume, 8vo, price 16s., cloth,
A CONCISE TREATISE ON THE
STATUTE LAW OF THE LIMITATIONS OF ACTIONS.
With an Appendix of Statutes, Copious References to English, Irish, and American Cases, and to the French Code, and a Copious Index.

By HENRY THOMAS BANNING, M.A.,
OF THE INNER TEMPLE, BARRISTER-AT-LAW.

"The work is decidedly valuable."—*Law Times.*
"Mr. Banning has adhered to the plan of printing the Acts in an appendix, and making his book a running treatise on the case-law thereon. The cases have evidently been investigated with care and digested with clearness and intellectuality."—*Law Journal.*

In 8vo, price 1s., sewed,
AN ESSAY ON THE
ABOLITION OF CAPITAL PUNISHMENT.
Embracing more particularly an Enunciation and Analysis of the Principles of Law as applicable to Criminals of the Highest Degree of Guilt.

By WALTER ARTHUR COPINGER,
OF THE MIDDLE TEMPLE, ESQ., BARRISTER-AT-LAW.

Sixth Edition, in 8vo, price 31s. 6d., cloth,
THE INDIAN CONTRACT ACT, No. IX., of 1872.
TOGETHER
WITH AN INTRODUCTION AND EXPLANATORY NOTES, TABLE OF CONTENTS, APPENDIX, AND INDEX.

By H. S. CUNNINGHAM AND H. H. SHEPHERD,
BARRISTERS-AT-LAW.

Second Edition, in 8vo, price 15s., cloth,

LEADING CASES and OPINIONS on INTERNATIONAL LAW

COLLECTED AND DIGESTED FROM
ENGLISH AND FOREIGN REPORTS, OFFICIAL DOCUMENTS, PARLIAMENTARY PAPERS, and other Sources.

With NOTES and EXCURSUS, Containing the Views of the Text-Writers on the Topics referred to, together with Supplementary Cases, Treaties, and Statutes; and Embodying an Account of some of the more important International Transactions and Controversies.

By PITT COBBETT, M.A., D.C.L.,
OF GRAY'S INN, BARRISTER-AT-LAW, PROFESSOR OF LAW, UNIVERSITY OF SYDNEY, N.S.W.

"The book is well arranged, the materials well selected, and the comments to the point. Much will be found in small space in this book."—*Law Journal.*

"The notes are concisely written and trustworthy. . . . The reader will learn from them a great deal on the subject, and the book as a whole seems a convenient introduction to fuller and more systematic works."—*Oxford Magazine.*

Second Edition, in royal 8vo. 1100 pages, price 45s., cloth,

STORY'S COMMENTARIES ON EQUITY JURISPRUDENCE.

Second English Edition, from the Twelfth American Edition.

By W. E. GRIGSBY, LL.D. (Lond.), D.C.L. (Oxon.),
AND OF THE INNER TEMPLE, BARRISTER-AT-LAW.

"It is high testimony to the reputation of Story, and to the editorship of Dr. Grigsby, that another edition should have been called for. . . . The work has been rendered more perfect by additional indices."—*Law Times.*

Second Edition, in 8vo, price 8s., cloth,

THE PARTITION ACTS, 1868 & 1876.

A Manual of the Law of Partition and of Sale, in Lieu of Partition. With the Decided Cases, and an Appendix containing Judgments and Orders. By W. GREGORY WALKER, B.A., of Lincoln's Inn, Barrister-at-Law.

"This is a very good manual—practical, clearly written, and complete. The subject lends itself well to the mode of treatment adopted by Mr. Walker, and in his notes to the various sections he has carefully brought together the cases, and discussed the difficulties arising upon the language of the different provisions."—*Solicitors' Journal.*

Second Edition, in 8vo, price 22s., cloth,

A TREATISE ON THE
LAW AND PRACTICE RELATING TO INFANTS.

By ARCHIBALD H. SIMPSON, M.A.,
OF LINCOLN'S INN, BARRISTER-AT-LAW, AND FELLOW OF CHRIST'S COLLEGE, CAMBRIDGE.

SECOND EDITION. By E. J. ELGOOD, B.C.L., M.A., of Lincoln's Inn, Barrister-at-Law.

"Mr. Simpson's book comprises the whole of the law relating to infants, both as regards their persons and their property, and we have not observed any very important omissions. The author has evidently expended much trouble and care upon his work, and has brought together, in a concise and convenient form, the whole of the subject down to the present time."—*Solicitors' Journal.*

"Its law is unimpeachable. We have detected no errors, and whilst the work might have been done more scientifically, in all question, a compendium of sound legal principles."—*Law Times.*

"Mr. Simpson has arranged the whole of the Law relating to Infants with much fulness of detail, and yet in comparatively little space. The result is due mainly to the businesslike condensation of his style. Fulness, however, has by no means been sacrificed to brevity, and, so far as we have been able to test it, the work omits no point of any importance, from the earliest cases to the last. In the essential qualities of clearness, completeness, and orderly arrangement it leaves nothing to be desired.

"Lawyers in doubt on any point of law or practice will find the information they require, if it is to be found at all, in Mr. Simpson's book, and a writer of whom this can be said may congratulate himself on having achieved a considerable success."
—*Law Magazine*, February, 1876.

In one volume, royal 8vo, 1877, price 30s., cloth,

THE DOCTRINES & PRINCIPLES OF THE LAW OF INJUNCTIONS.

By WILLIAM JOYCE,
OF LINCOLN'S INN, BARRISTER-AT-LAW.

"Mr. Joyce, whose learned and exhaustive work on 'The Law and Practice of Injunctions' has gained such a deservedly high reputation in the Profession, now brings out a valuable companion volume on the 'Doctrines and Principles' of this important branch of the Law. In the present work the Law is enunciated in its abstract rather than its concrete form, as few cases as possible being cited; while at the same time no statement of a principle is made unsupported by a decision, and for the most part the very language of the Courts has been adhered to. Written as it is by so acknowledged a master of his subject and with the conscientious carefulness that might be expected from him, this work cannot fail to prove of the greatest assistance alike to the Student—who wants to grasp principles freed from their superincumbent details—and to the practitioner, who wants to refresh his memory on points of doctrine amidst the oppressive details of professional work."—*Law Magazine and Review.*

BY THE SAME AUTHOR.

In two volumes, royal 8vo, 1872, price 70s., cloth,

THE LAW & PRACTICE OF INJUNCTIONS.

EMBRACING
ALL THE SUBJECTS IN WHICH COURTS OF EQUITY
AND COMMON LAW HAVE JURISDICTION.

By WILLIAM JOYCE,
OF LINCOLN'S INN, BARRISTER-AT-LAW.

REVIEWS.

"A work which aims at being so absolutely complete, as that of Mr. Joyce upon a subject which is of almost perpetual recurrence in the Courts, cannot fail to be a welcome offering to the profession, and doubtless, it will be well received and largely used, for it is as absolutely complete as it aims at being. .... This work is, therefore, eminently a work for the practitioner, being full of practical utility in every page, and every sentence, of it. .... We have to congratulate the profession on this new acquisition to a digest of the law, and the author on his production of a work of permanent utility and fame."—*Law Magazine and Review.*

"Mr. Joyce has produced, not a treatise, but a complete and compendious *exposition* of the Law and Practice of Injunctions both in equity and common law.
"Part III. is devoted to the practice of the Courts. *Contains an amount of valuable and technical matter nowhere else collected.*

"From these remarks it will be sufficiently perceived what elaborate and painstaking industry, as well as legal knowledge and ability has been necessary in the compilation of Mr. Joyce's work. No labour has been spared to save the practitioner labour, and no research has been omitted which could tend towards the elucidation and exemplification of the general principles of the Law and Practice of Injunctions."—*Law Journal.*

"He does not attempt to go an inch beyond that for which he has express written authority; he allows the cases to speak, and does not speak for them.
"The work is something more than a treatise on the Law of Injunctions. It gives us the general law on almost every subject to which the process of injunction is applicable. Not only English, but American decisions are cited, the aggregate number being 3,500, and the statutes cited 160, whilst the index is, we think, the most elaborate we have ever seen—occupying nearly 200 pages. The work is probably entirely exhaustive."—*Law Times.*

"This work, considered either as to its matter or manner of execution, is no ordinary work. It is a complete and exhaustive treatise both as to the law and the practice of granting injunctions. It must supersede all other works on the subject. The terse statement of the practice will be found of incalculable value. We know of no book as suitable to supply a knowledge of the law of injunctions to our common law friends as Mr. Joyce's exhaustive work. It is alike indispensable to members of the Common Law and Equity Bars. Mr. Joyce's great work would be a casket without a key unless accompanied by a good index. His index is very full and well arranged. We feel that this work is destined to take its place as a standard text-book, and *the* text-book on the particular subject of which it treats. The author deserves great credit for the very great labour bestowed upon it. The publishers, as usual, have acquitted themselves in a manner deserving of the high reputation they bear."—*Canada Law Journal.*

Third Edition, in 8vo, price 20s., cloth,

A TREATISE UPON
THE LAW OF EXTRADITION,
WITH THE CONVENTIONS UPON THE SUBJECT EXISTING BETWEEN ENGLAND AND FOREIGN NATIONS,
AND THE CASES DECIDED THEREON.
By SIR EDWARD CLARKE,
OF LINCOLN'S INN, S.-G., Q.C., M.P.

"Mr. Clarke's accurate and sensible book is the best authority to which the English reader can turn upon the subject of Extradition."—*Saturday Review*.
"The opinion we expressed of the merits of this work when it first appeared has been fully justified by the reputation it has gained. It is seldom we come across a book possessing so much interest to the general reader and at the same time furnishing so useful a guide to the lawyer."—*Solicitors' Journal*.
"The appearance of a second edition of this treatise does not surprise us. It is a useful book, well arranged and well written. A student who wants to learn the principles and practice of the law of extradition will be greatly helped by Mr. Clarke. Lawyers who have extradition business will find this volume an excellent book of reference. Magistrates who have to administer the extradition law will be greatly assisted by a careful perusal of 'Clarke upon Extradition.' This may be called a warm commendation, but those who have read the book will not say it is unmerited."—*Law Journal*.
THE TIMES of September 7, 1874, in a long article upon "Extradition Treaties," makes considerable use of this work and writes of it as "*Mr. Clarke's useful Work on Extradition*."

In 8vo, price 2s. 6d., cloth,
TABLES OF STAMP DUTIES
FROM 1815 TO 1878.
By WALTER ARTHUR COPINGER,
OF THE MIDDLE TEMPLE, ESQUIRE, BARRISTER-AT-LAW; AUTHOR OF "THE LAW OF COPYRIGHT IN WORKS OF LITERATURE AND ART," "INDEX TO PRECEDENTS IN CONVEYANCING," "TITLE DEEDS," &C.

"We think this little book ought to find its way into a good many chambers and offices."—*Solicitors' Journal*.
"This book, or at least one containing the same amount of valuable and well-arranged information, should find a place in every Solicitor's office. It is of especial value when examining the abstract of a large number of old title-deeds."—*Law Times*.
"His *Tables of Stamp Duties, from 1815 to 1878*, have already been tested in Chambers, and being now published, will materially lighten the labours of the profession in a tedious department, yet one requiring great care."—*Law Magazine and Review*.

In one volume, 8vo, price 14s., cloth,
TITLE DEEDS:
THEIR CUSTODY, INSPECTION, AND PRODUCTION, AT LAW, IN EQUITY, AND IN MATTERS OF CONVEYANCING,

Including Covenants for the Production of Deeds and Attested Copies; with an Appendix of Precedents, the Vendor and Purchaser Act, 1874, &c. &c. &c. By WALTER ARTHUR COPINGER, of the Middle Temple, Barrister-at-Law; Author of "The Law of Copyright" and "Index to Precedents in Conveyancing."

"The literary execution of the work is good enough to invite quotation, but the volume is not large, and we content ourselves with recommending it to the profession."—*Law Times*.
"A really good treatise on this subject must be essential to the lawyer: and this is what we have here. Mr. Copinger has supplied a much-felt want, by the compilation of this volume. We have not space to go into the details of the book; it appears well arranged, clearly written, and fully elaborated. With these few remarks we recommend his volume to our readers."—*Law Journal*.

Third Edition, in 8vo, considerably enlarged, price 36s., cloth,
THE LAW OF COPYRIGHT
In Works of Literature and Art; including that of the Drama, Music, Engraving, Sculpture, Painting, Photography, and Ornamental and Useful Designs; together with International and Foreign Copyright, with the Statutes relating thereto, and References to the English and American Decisions. By WALTER ARTHUR COPINGER, of the Middle Temple, Barrister-at-Law.

"Mr. Copinger's book is very comprehensive, dealing with every branch of his subject, and even extending to copyright in foreign countries. So far as we have examined, we have found all the recent authorities noted up with scrupulous care, and there is an unusually good index. These are merits which will, doubtless, lead to the placing of this edition on the shelves of the members of the profession whose business is concerned with copyright; and deservedly, for the book is one of considerable value."—*Solicitors' Journal*.

Third Edition, in One large Volume, 8vo, price 32s., cloth,

A MAGISTERIAL AND POLICE GUIDE:

BEING THE LAW
RELATING TO THE
PROCEDURE, JURISDICTION, AND DUTIES OF MAGISTRATES AND POLICE AUTHORITIES,
IN THE METROPOLIS AND IN THE COUNTRY.

With an Introduction showing the General Procedure before Magistrates both in Indictable and Summary Matters.

By HENRY C. GREENWOOD,
STIPENDIARY MAGISTRATE FOR THE DISTRICT OF THE STAFFORDSHIRE POTTERIES; AND

TEMPLE CHEVALIER MARTIN,
CHIEF CLERK TO THE MAGISTRATES AT LAMBETH POLICE COURT, LONDON;
AUTHOR OF "THE LAW OF MAINTENANCE AND DESERTION," "THE NEW FORMULIST," ETC.

Third Edition. Including the SESSION 52 & 53 Vict., and the CASES DECIDED in the SUPERIOR COURTS to the END OF THE YEAR 1889, *revised and enlarged,*

By TEMPLE CHEVALIER MARTIN.

"A second edition has appeared of Messrs. Greenwood and Martin's valuable and comprehensive magisterial and police Guide, a book which Justices of the peace should take care to include in their Libraries."—*Saturday Review.*

"Hence it is that we rarely light upon a work which commands our confidence, not merely by its research, but also by its grasp of the subject of which it treats. The volume before us is one of the happy few of this latter class, and it is on this account that the public favour will certainly wait upon it. We are moreover convinced that no effort has been spared by its authors to render it a thoroughly efficient and trustworthy guide."—*Law Journal.*

"Magistrates will find a valuable handbook in Messrs. Greenwood and Martin's 'Magisterial and Police Guide,' of which a fresh Edition has just been published."—*The Times.*

"A very valuable introduction, treating of proceedings before Magistrates, and largely of the Summary Jurisdiction Act, is in itself a treatise which will repay perusal. We expressed our high opinion of the Guide when it first appeared, and the favourable impression then produced is increased by our examination of this Second Edition."—*Law Times.*

"For the form of the work we have nothing but commendation. We may say we have here our ideal law book. . It may be said to omit nothing which it ought to contain."—*Law Times.*

"This handsome volume aims at presenting a comprehensive magisterial handbook for the whole of England. The mode of arrangement seems to us excellent, and is well carried out."—*Solicitors' Journal.*

"The *Magisterial and Police Guide,* by Mr. Henry Greenwood and Mr. Temple Martin, is a model work in its conciseness, and, so far as we have been able to test it, in completeness and accuracy. *It ought to be in the hands of all who, as magistrates or otherwise, have authority in matters of police.*"—*Daily News.*

"*This work is eminently practical, and supplies a real want. It plainly and concisely states the law on all points upon which Magistrates are called upon to adjudicate, systematically arranged, so as to be easy of reference. It ought to find a place on every Justice's table, and we cannot but think that its usefulness will speedily ensure for it as large a sale as its merits deserve.*"—*Midland Counties Herald.*

"The exceedingly arduous task of collecting together all the enactments on the subject has been ably and efficiently performed, and the arrangement is so methodical and precise that one is able to lay a finger on a Section of an Act almost in a moment. It is wonderful what a mass of information is comprised in so comparatively small a space. We have much pleasure in recommending the volume not only to our professional, but also to our general readers; nothing can be more useful to the public than an acquaintance with the outlines of magisterial jurisdiction and procedure."—*Sheffield Post.*

STEVENS & HAYNES, BELL YARD, TEMPLE BAR. 47

In one thick volume, 8vo, price 32s., cloth,

THE LAW OF RAILWAY COMPANIES.

Comprising the Companies Clauses, the Lands Clauses, the Railways Clauses Consolidation Acts, the Railway Companies Act, 1867, and the Regulation of Railways Act, 1868; with Notes of Cases on all the Sections, brought down to the end of the year 1868; together with an Appendix giving all the other material Acts relating to Railways, and the Standing Orders of the Houses of Lords and Commons; and a copious Index. By HENRY GODEFROI, of Lincoln's Inn, and JOHN SHORTT, of the Middle Temple, Barristers-at-Law.

In a handy volume, crown 8vo, 1870, price 10s. 6d., cloth,

THE LAW OF SALVAGE,

As administered in the High Court of Admiralty and the County Courts; with the Principal Authorities, English and American, brought down to the present time; and an Appendix, containing Statutes, Forms, Table of Fees, etc. By EDWYN JONES, of Gray's Inn, Barrister-at-Law.

In crown 8vo, price 4s., cloth,

A HANDBOOK OF THE

LAW OF PARLIAMENTARY REGISTRATION.

WITH AN APPENDIX OF STATUTES AND FULL INDEX.

By J. R. SEAGER, REGISTRATION AGENT.

In 8vo, price 5s., cloth,

THE LAW OF PROMOTERS OF PUBLIC COMPANIES.

By NEWMAN WATTS,

OF LINCOLN'S INN, BARRISTER-AT-LAW.

"Some recent cases in our law courts, which at the time attracted much public notice, have demonstrated the want of some clear and concise exposition of the powers and liabilities of promoters, and this task has been ably performed by Mr. Newman Watts."—*Investor's Guardian.*

"Mr. Watts has brought together all the leading decisions relating to promoters and directors, and has arranged the information in a very satisfactory manner, so as to readily show the rights of different parties and the steps which can be legally taken by promoters to further interests of new companies."—*Daily Chronicle.*

Second Edition, in One Vol., 8vo, price 12s., cloth,

A COMPENDIUM OF ROMAN LAW,

FOUNDED ON THE INSTITUTES OF JUSTINIAN; together with Examination Questions Set in the University and Bar Examinations (with Solutions), and Definitions of Leading Terms in the Words of the Principal Authorities. Second Edition. By GORDON CAMPBELL, of the Inner Temple, M.A., late Scholar of Exeter College, Oxford; M.A., LL.D., Trinity College, Cambridge; Author of "An Analysis of Austin's Jurisprudence, or the Philosophy of Positive Law."

In 8vo, price 7s. 6d., cloth,

TITLES TO MINES IN THE UNITED STATES,

WITH THE

STATUTES AND REFERENCES TO THE DECISIONS OF THE COURTS RELATING THERETO.

By W. A. HARRIS, B.A. OXON.,

OF LINCOLN'S INN, BARRISTER-AT-LAW; AND OF THE AMERICAN BAR.

INDEX

To the Names of Authors and Editors of Works enumerated in this Catalogue.

ALDRED (P. F.), page 21.
ARGLES (N.), 32. ASHWORTH (P. A.), 21.
ATTENBOROUGH (C. L.), 27.
BALDWIN (E. T.), 15.
BANNING (H. T.), 42
BEAL (E.), 32. BELLEWE (R.), 34.
BELLOT & WILLIS, 11.
BEVEN (T.), 8.
BLYTH (E. E.), 22.
BRICE (SEWARD), 16, 33.
BROOKE (Sir R.), 35.
BROOKS (W. J.), 13.
BROWN (ARCHIBALD), 20, 22, 26, 33, 40.
BROWNE (J. H. BALFOUR), 19.
BUCHANAN (J.), 38.
BUCKLEY (H. B.), 17.
BUCKNILL (T. T.), 34, 35.
CAMPBELL (GORDON), 47.
CAMPBELL (ROBERT), 9, 40.
CECIL (Lord R.), 11.
CHASTER (A. W.), 32. CHITTY (J. J. C.), 38.
CLARKE (EDWARD), 45.
CLAUSON (A. C.), 17.
COBBETT (PITT), 43.
COGHLAN (W. M.), 28.
COOKE (Sir G.), 35.
COOKE (HUGH), 10.
COPINGER (W. A.), 42, 45.
CORNER (R. J.), 10.
COTTERELL (J. N.), 28.
CRAIES (W. F.), 6, 9.
CUNNINGHAM (H. S.), 38, 42.
CUNNINGHAM (JOHN), 7.
CUNNINGHAM (T.), 34.
DANIEL (E. M.), 42.
DARLING (C. J.), 18.
DEANE (H. C.), 23.
DE BRUYN (D. P.), 38. DE WAL (J.), 38.
DIBDIN (L. T.), 10.
DUNCAN (J. A.), 33.
EDWARDS (W. D.), 16, 39.
ELGOOD (E. J.), 6, 18, 43.
ELLIOTT (G.), 14.
ERRINGTON (F. H. L.), 10.
EVANS (M. O.), 20.
EVERSLEY (W. P.), 9.
FINLASON (W. F.), 32.
FOA (E.), 11.
FOOTE (J. ALDERSON), 36.
FORBES (U. A.), 18.
FORSYTH (W.), 14. FROST (R.), 12.
GIBBS (F. W.), 10.
GODEFROI (H.), 47.
GREENWOOD (H. C.), 46.
GRIFFITHS (J. R.), 40.
GRIGSBY (W. E.), 43.
GROTIUS (HUGO), 38.
HALL (R. G.), 30.
HANSON (A.), 10.
HARDCASTLE (H.), 9.
HARRIS (SEYMOUR F.), 20, 27.
HARRIS (W. A.), 47.
HARRISON (J. C.), 23.
HARWOOD (R. G.), 10.

HAZLITT (W.), 29.
HIGGINS (C.), 30.
HOUSTON (J.), 32.
HUDSON (A. A.), 12. HURST (J.), 11.
INDERMAUR (JOHN), 24, 25, 28.
INDERWICK, 11.
JONES (E.), 47. JOYCE (W.), 44.
KAY (JOSEPH), 17.
KELKE (W. H.), 6.
KELYNG (Sir J.), 35.
KELYNGE (W.), 35.
KOTZÉ (J. G.), 38.
LLOYD (EYRE), 13.
LORENZ (C. A.), 38.
LOVELAND (R. L.), 30, 34, 35.
MAASDORP (A. F. S.), 38.
MACASKIE (S. C.), 7.
MANSFIELD (Hon. J. W.), 17.
MARCH (JOHN), 35.
MARCY (G. N.), 26.
MARTIN (TEMPLE C.), 7, 46.
MATTINSON (M. W.), 7.
MAY (H. W.), 29.
MAYNE (JOHN D.), 31, 38.
MELLOR (F. H.), 10.
MENZIES (W.), 38. MOORE (S. A.), 30.
NORTON-KYSHE, 40.
O'MALLEY (E. L.), 33.
PAVITT (A.), 32. PEILE (C. J.), 7.
PEMBERTON (L. L.), 18, 32.
PHIPSON (S. L.), 20.
PORTER (J. B.), 6.
REILLY (F. S.), 29. RENTON (A. W.), 10.
RINGWOOD (R.), 13, 15, 29
SALKOWSKI (C.), 14.
SALMOND (J. W.), 13.
SAVIGNY (F. C. VON), 20.
SCOTT (C. E.), 32.
SEAGER (J. R.), 47.
SHORT (F. H.), 10, 41.
SHORTT (JOHN), 47.
SHOWER (Sir B.), 34.
SIMPSON (A. H.), 43.
SLATER (J.), 7.
SMITH (EUSTACE), 23, 39.
SMITH (F. J.), 6.
SMITH (LUMLEY), 31.
SNELL (E. H. T.), 22.
STORY, 43.
TARRING (C. J.), 26, 41, 42.
TASWELL-LANGMEAD, 21.
THOMAS (ERNEST C.), 28.
TYSSEN (A. D.), 39.
VAN DER KEESEL (D. G.), 38.
VAN LEEUWEN, 38. VAN ZYL, 38.
WAITE (W. T.), 22.
WALKER (W. G.), 6, 18, 43.
WATTS (C. N.), 47.
WERTHEIMER (J.), 32.
WHITEFORD (F. M.), 33.
WHITFIELD (E. E.), 14.
WILLIAMS (E. S.), 7.
WILLIS (W.), 14.
WORTHINGTON (S. W.), 29.

www.ingramcontent.com/pod-product-compliance
Lightning Source LLC
Chambersburg PA
CBHW032148160426
43197CB00008B/811